Smiling Pages

Motivational Tales to Brighten Your Day

Other Books by Sharad Gupta

1. A Bunch of Thoughts on Pure Living
2. Bliss: A Treasure-Trove of Smilies
3. Tequila of Life: Inspirational Tales
4. Ecstasy: Delightful Tales from Life

Smiling Pages

Motivational Tales to Brighten Your Day

Compiled and Edited by

Sharad Gupta

ALLIED PUBLISHERS PVT. LTD.

Noida • Mumbai • Kolkata • Chennai • Bangalore

ALLIED PUBLISHERS PRIVATE LIMITED

D-5, Sector-2, **Noida**–201 301
Ph. Nos.: 0120-4320295/2542557/4352866
E-mail: delhi.books@alliedpublishers.com

17 Chittaranjan Avenue, **Kolkata**–700072
Ph.: 033-22129618 • E-mail: cal.books@alliedpublishers.com

15 J.N. Heredia Marg, Ballard Estate, **Mumbai**–400001
Ph.: 022-42126969 • E-mail: mumbai.books@alliedpublishers.com

No. 25/10, Commander-in-Chief Road, Ethiraj Lane (Next to Post Office)
Egmore, **Chennai**–600008
Ph.: 044-28223938 • E-mail: chennai.books@alliedpublishers.com

P.B. No. 9932, No. 15, 3rd Floor (Next to Vijaya Bank), 5th Cross, Gandhinagar, Karnataka, **Bangalore**–560009. Ph.: 080-41530285/22386239
E-mail: bngl.books@alliedpublishers.com

Website: www.alliedpublishers.com

ISBN: 978-93-89934-84-7

Life may not be the party we hoped for,
but while we are here we might as well dance.

* * *

There is not enough darkness in the whole world to put out the light of a small candle. No man is so poor as not to have many of these small candles. When these are lighted, darkness goes away and a touch of wonder remains.

Published by Sunil Sachdev and printed by Ravi Sachdev
at Allied Publishers Pvt. Ltd., D-5, Sector-2, Noida–201 301

Preface

In a world filled with diverse experiences and perspectives, inspiration can come from anywhere. This collection of stories aims to transcend age boundaries, offering motivating tales that resonate with readers of all ages. Within these pages, you'll find stories of wit, wisdom, courage, resilience and hope that will leave you inspired and eager to make a positive impact in your life.

This book is not intended to preach ethics, religion or moral issues. Instead, its purpose is to act as a tonic to nourish and rejuvenate your soul, as words that enlighten the soul are more precious than jewels. Each story leads to a point of illumination, evoking an original, unmeditated response that readers are sure to treasure. This book is designed to be a pathway of life that might lead to one's highest good.

In an era where negativity often dominates the headlines, it's more important than ever to share stories that uplift and inspire. This book is a testament to the human spirit's capacity for resilience, compassion and innovation. Through these pages, I invite you to embark on a journey of discovery, exploring the countless ways in which ordinary people have achieved extra-ordinary things.

Stories have the power to unite us, to make us feel seen and heard, and to inspire us to be our best selves. This book brings together a diverse range of tales that celebrate the human spirit, highlighting moments of triumph, kindness and determination. Whether you're 16 or 96, these stories will remind you of the transformative power of inspiration and the boundless potential within each of us.

I dedicate this book to my precious grandchildren, Yuvein and Yana, who bring immense joy and light to my life. They embody the innocence, wonder and joy that these stories aim to capture. Yuvein, at four years old, your curiosity and enthusiasm inspires me to share tales that spark imagination and fuel dreams. And Yana, in your first tender months, your presence reminds me of the purity and magic of life. I love you both more than words can express.

As I share these stories and experiences with the world, I hope that you will always remember that your dreams are worth chasing, your voices are worth hearing, and your love is worth sharing. May this book be a reminder of the boundless love and support that surrounds you, and may you grow up to be compassionate, courageous and brilliant individuals who make a positive impact on the world.

I would like to acknowledge that some of the stories in this collection have been sourced from unknown sources, including oral traditions and folklore. While I have made every effort to verify the accuracy and origins of these stories, some may remain unknown or unverified. I express my gratitude to the many storytellers, authors and tradition-keepers who have contributed to the rich cultural heritage that underlies these timeless inspirational tales.

As you read through these pages, I hope you'll find yourself inspired by the courage, creativity and kindness of the individuals featured within. May these stories spark a sense of wonder, curiosity and hope within you, and may you carry their inspiration with you long after you finish reading.

Happy reading!

Contents

Choices

It was a hot sunny summer day. A tired man was walking through a desert. Not a drop of water was left with him. He felt helpless and thought he would certainly die. Still keeping a ray of hope in mind, he was moving forward. Suddenly, he saw a hut. He wondered if he was hallucinating. Gathering his last drop of energy, he reached the hut. There was no one there. His heart skipped a beat, when he saw a hand pump in the hut. What a blessing! But his over-excitement soon vanished when he could not extract even a drop of water out of it.

He was about to give up in despair. Then he watched the room carefully. Unexpectedly, he noticed a bottle of water in the corner of the room and a piece of paper under that bottle. It was written, "Use this water to start the pump. Do not forget to refill this bottle and re-cork it properly." At the bottom there was a map on which the next location of getting water was pointed out, which was far from the hut.

And here the dilemma started! What should he do now? He stopped and thought for a moment. He can simply drink that bottle of water and save his life instantly. But, in that case, he would not be able to carry along any water on his way ahead. Also, anyone else who would turn up there will not get even a drop to save his life. But what if the pump did not work?

In any case, he had to take a risk—sooner or later. Uncertainty of the result gave birth to confusion in his mind. His hands were trembling. He controlled his emotions, applied his reasoning, and opted for the second choice. To his great delight, cool refreshing water came out of the pump. Hurray! He shouted at the top of his voice. He drank it like a thirsty crow, refilled the bottle and corked it as per instruction. Moreover, he added under the instruction, "Believe me, it works." He also refilled his containers, rested for a while, and started his journey once again with a smile on his face.

Perfection

One day in the marketplace, Mullah Nasruddin encountered an old friend who was happily married for over a decade. The friend asked Nasruddin whether he had ever considered marriage.

Nasruddin replied that years ago he had wanted to and had set out to find the perfect woman. First he travelled to Damascus, where he found a perfectly gracious and beautiful woman, but discovered she was lacking a spiritual side. Then his travels took him farther to Isfahan, where he met a woman who was deeply spiritual and beautiful as well, but unfortunately they did not communicate well together.

"Finally, in Cairo I found her" he said, "She was the ideal woman, spiritual, gracious, communicative and beautiful, perfect in every way."

"Well" asked the friend, "Did you then marry her?"

"No", answered Nasruddin, "Unfortunately, she was looking for the perfect man."

> *I had a blind date yesterday evening. However, I was concerned—What will I do if she's really unattractive? I'll be stuck with her all evening. I consulted an experienced friend. He told me that there is an app for that. It's called "Mom, are you Ok". It schedules your phone to ring just after you meet her. If you like her, you ignore the call. If you want to cut short the date, you answer with, "Mom, what's the matter? Are you okay?" Apparently, it works every time. So I knocked on the girl's door. As it turned out, I had nothing to worry about. She was stunningly beautiful! I couldn't get over how attractive she was. Just as I was about to introduce myself, her phone rang! She answered it and said, "Mom, what's the matter? Are you okay?"*

From the Diary of a Gynaecologist

I started my first job at a hospital in Alibaug. One afternoon an injured woman came, who was pregnant after eleven years of marriage. A bull roaming around the streets of Alibaug had knocked her, and had gored her stomach with its horn. It was a scary sight, with part of the woman's stomach injured and a baby's hand protruding out of the crack of the uterine wall.

I was in a state of panic. Fortunately, the mother's life was not in danger, and her stomach wound was not severe. But to sew up the wall of the uterus was unthinkable, as it was impossible to put back the child's hand inside.

The family's instruction was clear, "Save the mother's life." But how could I ignore the plea of that tiny hand, seemingly reaching out for help.

The operation theatre had a minimal staff. Apart from me there were two nurses, a compounder and a helper whose job was to sterilize tools. He was middle aged and an alcoholic, but extremely sincere and efficient in his work, for which the entire staff tolerated him. In the OT, I observed that he was standing quietly behind, observing the proceedings. After healing the stomach wound, how do I get that little hand inside was beyond my bookish knowledge. The creator had made the uterine wall so strong that it cannot be opened easily. No option came to my mind except to perform surgery.

At this point the helper, who was silently watching, came up to me and whispered in my ear, "Saheb, there is a way that the hand will automatically move in." I stared at him. Time was precious. I didn't know why, but my inner conscience made me ask him what he had in mind. He said "Heat the injection needle and touch the hand, it will immediately go back." Having no other option, I agreed to his crazy suggestion. I prayed to God in my heart and asked for a hundred apologies from that little one, gathered courage, warmed the needle and pricked it lightly. The miracle happened at once! The baby's hand immediately withdrew back inside with a jerk. Further work was easy. I did the dressing of the uterine wall.

Two months later, the woman safely delivered the baby in the same hospital and that little baby was smiling right in my arms.

Doctor said: We can remove those stretch marks from your stomach.

She smiled and replied: Never. It's my baby's first drawing.

* * *

In a day, when you don't come across any problems—you can be sure that you are traveling in a wrong path.

* * *

Challenges are high

The Dreams are new

The World out there

Is waiting for you.

Dare to Dream

Dare to Try

No Goal is too distant

No Star is too high.

The Ultimate Banker

Syndicate Bank merged with Canara Bank on 1st April 2020. With bank mergers taking place and banks losing their identity, here is a little-known story of a once-private Syndicate Bank, which started with a 25 paise deposit.

There are three key reasons why Syndicate Bank is important in the evolution of India as a wealth generator and for working towards the upliftment of masses.

First, it was born out of a belief that an innovative person cannot really generate wealth for himself on a sustainable basis unless he works out a way to make his community wealthy as well.

Secondly, it was the only large bank in India to locate its headquarters in a rural area—in the 1930s Manipal was still a village.

Thirdly, its promoters knew about how wealth could be found at the bottom of the pyramid.

At a time when all banks insisted on Rs 5 as the minimum deposit amount to open an account, Syndicate's promoters opened accounts with just 25 paise.

The bank itself was a brain child of Tonse Madhava Ananth Pai, who went to Bangalore to study medicine. He excelled in his studies, and after earning his license to practice medicine, he went back home to the fishing village of Maple.

He asked his parents if he could go to Japan for further studies, but was sternly told by his mother that he should stay in the village and practice medicine for the welfare of the people he grew up with. That broke the boy's heart. He yearned to continue his studies. Moreover, he knew that a fishing village would provide him neither money, nor the intellectual challenge.

His concerns were validated. In six months' time, he confirmed that a fishing village had only colds, fevers, diarrhea, dysentery and indigestion as regular ailments.

He tried persuading his parents one more time to let him go overseas for further studies. Once again, he was rebuffed. His relatives would talk of how the boy would go to sleep sobbing into his pillow crying over the unfairness of life.

And one day, he had his Eureka moment. He realized that one reason why he was not earning enough was because the people around him were also not earning enough. Could he change that? He began strategising a social revolution that India had never seen or imagined.

He knew, as a doctor, that children are brought to doctors invariably by mothers, seldom by fathers. So, he focused on the women who came to him. He began urging them not to let their children end up like their fathers who were good only for fishing and then getting drunk when they returned home. The cleaning of the fish, selling them, managing provisions, balancing incomes with expenses was left to women. If there was any surplus money, the men demanded it, and got drunk with that money.

So, he urged the women to save. But they told him that there wasn't enough money for saving. He would then ask them to show how much money they had. They would show him a few coins. He would gently take 25 paise coins from each woman and tell her to start with this.

He kept two notebooks for each woman—one with him and other with the woman. He told them that he would send his compounder over to their house every day when the husband was not around. If they could save 25 paise, the amount would be registered in both the notebooks.

The scheme, backed by constant persuasions and exhortations, worked. Women began saving. In a few months, Pai realized he had more than a thousand rupees—which translates into a few lakhs using today's valuation. The 25 paise deposit scheme came to be known as the Pygmy Deposit Scheme.

It was time to go to phase II of the plan. He told them that their children were falling ill very frequently because they consumed only fish and rice. He urged them to give the children a glass of milk every day. That was impossible. A glass of milk was unaffordable. So Pai urged them to buy a cow for their houses. They laughed, "We cannot afford a glass of milk, and you want us to buy a cow?" Pai gently told them that he could finance the cows for the women.

And repayment was also painless, he explained. "Just give your child a glass of milk, and I shall purchase the rest of the milk from you and adjust the cost of the cow. You don't have to do anything else."

It took a while to persuade the first woman. But when she agreed, it was a game of "me too". Within a short while, there were so many cows in the village that Pai could not purchase all their milk. He therefore formed a milk cooperative.

To handle the amount of money coming in he started a bank—Canara Industrial and Banking Syndicate Ltd—with its headquarters in Manipal. The first branch of the bank started its operations in 1925 at Udupi in Karnataka. By 1937, it had secured its membership as a clearing house in Mumbai.

He then started a weavers' cooperative, which too was financed by the bank.

Then to benefit the community he founded schools, then colleges and then institutions that taught engineering and medicine. This later became the prestigious Manipal Educational Complex.

To grow the bank, Pai used to look around for good businessmen, who had the ability and urge to grow and willingness to repay the amounts borrowed.

In one of his travels, he met a trader, whom he helped get a yarn license from the government. This businessman was Dhirubhai Ambani. And that is why a member of the Pai family remained on the board of Reliance Industries as long as he was alive.

Syndicate Bank used to be the lead agent for all loans syndicated by Reliance even though they did not have the largest share.

Ananth is also the name of Dhirubai's grandson—the name was apparently given by Dhirubhai as he held Ananth Pai in great esteem.

Unfortunately, this is a story that most management schools do not teach.

The fragrance of flowers spreads only in the direction of the wind. But the goodness of a person spreads in all directions.

* * *

A candle loses nothing if it is used to light another one.

* * *

The purpose of life is a life of purpose.

* * *

So often in life we cultivate a talent or two and then ride on these few talents through the rest of our lives. That is selling ourselves short. We are created as multitalented beings, and we should cultivate our versatility.

The great pleasure in life is doing what people say you cannot do. But a greater pleasure is doing things you previously thought you could not do.

How fulfilling is to be versatile! And you can be.

Does Evil Exist

In a philosophy class, the professor posed a profound question, "Does evil exist?"

One student took permission to ask a counter question. The student asked, "Does cold exist?"

The Professor replied, "Yes! Don't you feel cold dear?"

The student respectfully disagreed, "I'm sorry Sir, but you are mistaken. Cold is a complete absence of heat. There is no cold, it is only an absence of heat."

The student posed another question, "Does darkness exist?"

Professor replied, "Yes!"

The student respectfully disagreed again, "You are again wrong Sir. There is no such thing as darkness. It is actually the absence of light. Sir, we always study light and heat, but not cold and darkness."

"Similarly, evil does not exist. Actually, it is the absence of love, caring, compassion and righteousness. The evil remains only until it is overcome by good, but the good remains forever."

The name of the student was Swami Vivekananda.

Do you know the real identity of those around you? There is a story about an emperor who received a nightingale as a gift. He had never heard of this kind of bird, and to him it looked small, dull and unimpressive. He was about to have the cage and the bird removed, when the nightingale began to sing and its true identity was revealed. It became a prized possession of the emperor for times to come.

The Art of Listening

Viktor Frankl, one of the great psychiatrists of the twentieth century, survived the death camps of Nazi Germany. His highly influential book, *Man's Search for Meaning*, is one of those life-changing books that everyone should read. Frankl once told the story of a woman who called him in the middle of the night to inform him that she was about to commit suicide. Frankl kept her on the phone and helped her work through her depression, giving her reason after reason to carry on living. Finally she promised she would not take her life, and she kept her promise.

When they later met, Frankl asked which reason had persuaded her to live.

"None of them", she replied.

What then influenced her to go on living, he pressed.

Her answer was simple, it was Frankl's willingness to listen to her in the middle of the night. A world in which there was someone ready to listen to another's pain, seemed to her a world in which it was worthwhile to live.

Often, it is not the brilliant argument that makes the difference. Sometimes the small act of listening is the greatest gift we can give.

> *When the two ears are put side by side, it forms the shape of the heart.*
>
> *Interestingly, the word 'ear' sits right in the middle of the word 'heart' (h-ear-t).*
>
> *The ear is the way to the heart.*
>
> *So, if you want someone's heart, learn to listen.*

Out of the Box Solution

A big factory was being built in Kerala when a grave problem arose during the construction of that plant. The problem was that a really heavy machine had to be placed at the bottom of a deep pit built in the plant, but the weight of the machine posed a challenge.

The machine arrived at the site but how to get it down in the 30 feet deep pit had become a big problem. If not installed properly, both the foundation and the machine could be severely damaged.

Now, this was a time when cranes that could lift very heavy weights were not available everywhere. The ones available could probably lift the machine, but to land it in the deep pit was beyond their capacity.

Finally, the company constructing the plant gave up, and issued a tender to find a solution to this problem. In response, a lot of people sent their offers to fit this machine in the pit. Their quotes ranged from 10 to 15 lakh rupees to complete the work.

There was a gentleman among those people, who asked the company, "If the machine gets drenched in water, will there be any problem?" The company replied that "it will not make any difference to the machine."

After that, he also filled the tender. When all the offers were seen, that person had asked for only 5 lakh rupees for completing the work. So obviously, the job of setting up the machine was given to him.

The day finally came. Every employee, manager, even the boss of the company and everyone around were curious to know how that man would do this work. He had not even done any preparation on the site.

Well, on the decided time, a lot of trucks started reaching the site. All those trucks were loaded with ice slabs. The ice slabs were unloaded and filled into the pit. When the pit was completely filled with ice, they moved the machine and placed it atop the ice slabs. After this, a portable water pump was switched on and a pipe was inserted in the pit so that the water could be taken out. The ice melted, the water kept pouring out, and the machine started going down.

The work was completed within 4–5 hours and the total cost came to less than Rs. 1 lakh. The machine fitted perfectly and the man made a 4 times profit.

An underwear manufacturing company was having a tough time with stock theft.

On departure for home, bags of all workers were searched and everything always seemed okay. All security measures one can think of were put in place.

Supervisor was alerted but still no one was caught and stock continued to disappear.

Next, all workers, including the top management were checked on departure, each wearing just one underwear, and no one was caught with more than one pair.

Then....

One day, the supervisor advised security to check all workers on their arrival ...

And the case was solved!

How to be Rich

When I was doing my Engineering, there was a Professor whose lectures used to be heavily attended since he had an interesting way to teach and explain the concepts. One day, in the class, he explained the relationship of Zero and Infinity.

He said that if we take the diameter of the Earth as compared to distance between Earth and Sun, the diameter of earth can be said to be zero since it is too small.

However, when we compare the same diameter of Earth with the size of a grain, diameter of Earth can be said to be infinite.

Hence, he concluded that the same thing can be Zero and Infinite at the same time, depending on the context, or our matrix of comparison.

He further elaborated that relationship between richness and poverty is similar to the relationship between infinity and zero.

It all depends on the scale of comparison with our wants.

If our income is more than our wants, we are rich.

If our wants are more than our income, we are poor.

I consider myself rich because my wants are far less than my income. I have become rich not so much by acquiring lots of money, but by progressively reducing my wants.

If you can reduce your wants, you too can become rich at this very moment.

Life is 10% what you make it and 90% how you take it!

A New Lease of Life

A businessman was deep in debt and could see no way out. Creditors were closing in on him. Suppliers were demanding payment. He sat on a park bench, head in hands, wondering if anything could save his company from bankruptcy. Suddenly an old man appeared before him. "I can see that something is troubling you," he said. After listening to the businessman's woes, the old man said, "I believe I can help you." He asked the man his name, wrote out a cheque, and pushed it into his hand saying, "Take this money. Meet me here exactly one year from now, and you can pay me back at that time." The businessman saw in his hand a cheque for $ 500,000, signed by Henry Ford, then one of the richest men in the world! "I can erase my money worries in an instant!" He realised. But instead, the businessman decided to put the uncashed cheque in his safe. Just knowing it was there might give him the strength to work out a way to save his business, he thought. With renewed optimism, he negotiated better deals and extended terms of payment. He closed several big deals. Within a few months, he was out of debt and making money once again.

Exactly one year later, he returned to the park with the uncashed cheque. At the agreed-upon time, the old man appeared. But just as the executive was about to hand back the cheque and share his success story, a nurse came running up and grabbed the old man. "I'm so glad I caught him." She said. "I hope he hasn't been bothering you. He's always escaping from the mental asylum and telling people he's Henry Ford." And she led the old man away by the arm. The astonished businessman just stood there, stunned. All year long he'd been wheeling and dealing, buying and selling, convinced he had half a million dollars behind him. Suddenly, he realised that it wasn't the money, real or imagined, that had turned his life around. It was his newfound self-confidence that gave him the power to achieve anything he ever imagined.

The Two Falcons

Once there was a king who received a gift of two magnificent falcons from Arabia. They were the most beautiful birds he had ever seen. He gave the precious birds to his head falconer to be trained. Months passed and one day the head falconer informed the king that though one of the falcons was flying majestically, soaring high in the sky, the other bird had not moved from its branch since the day it had arrived.

The king summoned healers and sorcerers from all the land to tend to the falcon, but no one could make the bird fly. Having tried everything else, the king thought to himself, "May be I need someone more familiar with the countryside to understand the nature of this problem." So he instructed his court to get a farmer. In the morning, the king was thrilled to see the falcon soaring high above the palace gardens. He asked the farmer, "How did you make the falcon fly?"

With head bowed, the farmer said to the king, "It was very easy, your highness. I simply cut the branch of the tree where the bird was sitting."

Moral: We are all made to fly to realise our incredible potential as human beings. But instead of doing that, we sit on our branches, clinging to the things that are familiar to us.

The possibilities are endless, but for most of us, they remain undiscovered. We conform to the familiar, the comfortable, and the mundane. So for the most part, our lives are mediocre instead of exciting, thrilling and fulfilling.

So let us learn to destroy the branch of fear we cling to and free ourselves to the glory of flight!

> *Comfort zones are cosy graves, where potential goes to die, so dare to step out and rise.*

Urgently Needed...

Not Blood,
but
An Electrician,
to restore the joyful current between people, who do not speak to each other anymore.

An Optician,
to change the outlook of people.

An Artist,
to draw a smile on everyone's face.

A Civil Engineer,
to build bridges between neighbours.

A Gardener,
to cultivate good thoughts.

A Plumber,
to clear the choked and blocked mindsets.

A Scientist,
to rediscover compassion.

A Language Teacher,
for better communication with each other.

And Last but not the least,

A Maths Teacher,
for all of us to relearn how to count on each other.

Play the Battle Drums

A king had many elephants, but one elephant was very powerful, obedient, sensible and skillful in everything, especially his fighting skills. In many wars, he was sent on the battlefield and he used to return only after getting victory for the king. Therefore, he was the most loved elephant of the king.

Time went by and there came a time when the elephant started getting old. Now he was not able to perform as before. The king did not even send him to the battlefield but he still remained as a part of the king's cavalry.

One day, the elephant went to a lake to drink water, but unfortunately his feet got stuck in the quicksand there and he began to sink. He tried a lot, but could not free himself. People came to know from the sound of his screams that the elephant was in trouble. The news of the trapped elephant reached the king. Lots of people, including the king, gathered around the lake and made various efforts to get him out. But alas, even after trying for a long time, there was no way out.

At that time, Gautama Buddha was passing by. He stopped and learnt about the brave deeds of the elephant and then suggested to the king that the battle drums should be played around the lake. The listeners felt bewildered at the bizarre suggestion as to how the trapped elephant would come out by playing the battle drums. But they could not say anything to Gautam Buddha and started playing the drums. As soon as the drums of war started ringing, there was a change in the gestures, behaviour and determination of the troubled elephant. At first, the elephant slowly stood up and then gradually used his force and intelligence and before long, came out of the mud on his own, astonishing everyone. Gautama Buddha smiled and said, "There was no lack of physical ability in the elephant, but only the need to infuse motivation and will."

Miracle

A certain company had a tradition of holding a party and a lottery every new year. There were three hundred people in the company. Each employee contributed three hundred rupees. In other words, a total of ninety thousand rupees were raised. The winner was to take all the money home.

On the day of the lottery draw, office was filled with a lively atmosphere. Everyone wrote their names on the slips of paper and put them in the lottery box. However, a young man Akshat hesitated when he wrote. He knew that the company's cleaning lady Asha's frail and sickly son was going to have an operation but she did not have the required money to pay for it, which made her quite troubled. So, even though he knew that the chance of winning was slim, he wrote the name of the cleaner lady on the slip.

The tense moment came. The boss vigorously shook the lottery box, and finally drew out a chit. Akshat kept praying in his heart, hoping against hope that Asha wins the prize. Then the boss announced the winner's name. A miracle happened! The winner turned out to be Asha. Cheers broke out in the office, and Asha hurriedly rushed to the stage to accept the award. She almost burst into tears and said, "I am so fortunate and blessed! With this money, now my son has hope!"

Just out of curiosity, Akshat picked the lottery box and took out a chit and opened it casually. The name on it was also the name of the cleaning lady! Akshat was very surprised. He took out several chits one after another. Although the handwriting on them was different, the name was always the same—the cleaning lady's. Akshat's eyes were filled with tears and he clearly understood that it was a new year miracle, but the miracle did not fall from sky, compassionate colleagues were required to create it.

Audit Objection

Army personnel are entitled to an additional quantity of rum if it is taken at a certain altitude in the Himalayan region. A unit of Jat regiment was posted at a hilly location and drew the additional quota of rum.

After verification, the Audit Department came to the conclusion that the height of the location falls short by 5 feet from the height prescribed for additional rum entitlement. Hence as the unit had already consumed additional rum without entitlement, the members of the unit must pay back the cost of rum consumed.

Official memo to this effect was received by the CO of the unit. CO replied, "Ours is a formation of Jat regiment where the height of each jawan is more than 6 ft. We further undertake that all rum has been consumed in standing position only, thereby at a height more than the prescribed limit for free entitlement."

The audit objection was dropped.

This incident is about two brilliant business communities. Once a Sindhi bought a well from a Marwari. The next day while on his way to market he met the Marwari who told him "I have sold the well to you but not the water. If you use the water you will have to pay for it."

The Sindhi replied, "I was in fact planning to come to your place and ask you to remove the water, otherwise you will have to pay the rent for storing it in my well."

Nature is a Great Teacher

In the 1990s Japanese faced a particularly difficult challenge. When their high-speed trains entered a tunnel, they created pressure waves that reached other end of tunnel at the speed of sound. When the air exited the tunnel it created a loud sonic boom that was heard even 400 meters away, causing discomfort to people living in those areas. To mitigate this noise pollution, the trains were run at a lower speed.

Engineers looking for a solution to this problem were repeatedly frustrated. There was a keen bird watcher among them. He noticed that Kingfisher enters the water without making a splash when hunting for its prey. He thought that this could provide a solution. From the research that followed, it became clear that the Kingfisher's long beak and the round cross-section of its head enabled it to make a splash-less entry into the water.

Japanese used this information to re-design their Shinkansen 500 series with a beak like front and a round cross-section. The resulting sonic boom was much quieter and well below the norms set by the Japanese government. Not just that, the new trains had 30% less air resistance, consumed 13% less energy and could go a lot faster.

> *The illiterate of the present century will not be those who cannot read and write, but those who cannot learn, unlearn, and relearn.*
>
> * * *
>
> *If you have an apple and I have an apple and we exchange these apples then you and I will still each have one apple. But if you have an idea and I have an idea and we exchange these ideas, then each of us will have two ideas.*

Moment

In a forest, a pregnant deer is about to give birth to a baby. It finds a remote grass field nearby a river and slowly goes there, thinking it would be safe. As she moves cautiously, she gets labour pain.

At the same moment, dark clouds gather around that area and lightning starts a forest fire. Turning left, she sees a hunter who is aiming an arrow at her from a distance. As she tries to move towards right, she spots a hungry lion approaching towards her.

What can the pregnant deer do, as she is already under labour pain?

What do you think will happen?

Will the deer survive?

Will it give birth to a fawn?

Will the fawn survive?

Or

Will everything be burnt by the forest fire?

Can the deer go left? No, the hunter's arrow is pointing at her.

Can she go right? No, the hungry lion is approaching her.

Can she move up? No, there the forest is on fire.

Can she move down? No, that is where the fierce river is.

She does nothing. She just focuses on giving birth to a new LIFE.

The sequence of events that happen at that fraction of a second are as follows:

In a spur of a *moment*, a lightning strikes, and blinds the eyes of the hunter!

At that *moment*, he releases the arrow, missing and zipping past the deer, hitting and injuring the lion badly!

At that *moment*, it starts to rain heavily and puts out the forest fire!

At that *moment*, the deer gives birth to a healthy fawn!

In our life too, there are *moments of choice* when we all have to deal with negative thoughts from all sides. Some thoughts are so powerful they overcome us, and make us clueless.

Anything can happen in a *moment* in life. The priority of the deer, in that given *moment*, was simply giving birth to a baby, because life is precious!

We must accept finite disappointment, but never lose infinite hope.

* * *

In any moment of decision, the best thing you can do is the right thing, the next best thing is the wrong thing, and the worst thing you can do is nothing.

* * *

There is not enough darkness in the whole world to put out the light of a small candle. No man is so poor as not to have many of these small candles. When these are lighted, darkness goes away and a touch of wonder remains.

* * *

In the depth of winter, I finally learned that within me there lay an invincible summer.

Buy One, Get One Free

'Buy one, get one free' may be a marketing gimmick. But it is true in real life when we harbour certain emotions.

We get angry and acidity comes free.

We become jealous and get headache free.

We acquire hatred and get ulcer free.

We gain stress and get blood pressure free, and so on.

Conversely,

If we earn trust, we get friendship free.

If we do regular exercise, we get health free.

If we achieve peace, we get prosperity free.

If we are honest, we get sleep free.

If we are loving, we get all good virtues free.

May you be blessed with the wisdom to make choices that lead you to a healthy and purposeful life!

> ***Best Exercise.... is Walking....***
>
> *A lot of 'walking away' will do your life good.*
>
> *'Walk away' from arguments that lead you to anger.*
>
> *'Walk away' from people who deliberately put you down.*
>
> *'Walk away' from any thought that reduces your worth.*
>
> *'Walk away' from failures and fears that stifle your dreams.*
>
> *The more you 'walk away' from things that poison your soul, the happier your life will be.*
>
> *Practise 'Walking' towards Happiness.*

Attitude

Three old men were sitting in a park, discussing the inevitable—death. One man of eighty-three said, "When I die, I would like to be buried alongside Abraham Lincoln, the greatest man, loved by all."

Another said, "I would like to be buried next to Albert Einstein, the greatest scientist, humanitarian, philosopher, lover of peace."

Then they both looked at the third, who was ninety-three. He said, "I would like to be buried adjacent to Angelina Jolie."

They both felt annoyed, angry and they said, "But she is still alive."

That old man retorted, "So am I!"

Your attitude determines your altitude.

* * *

On an old man's shirt was written a sentence "I am not 80 years old; I am sweet 16 with 64 years of experience." That is attitude.

* * *

A person once went for an interview in a very reputed company. While entering the room, he slipped and fell on the ground. Documents scattered all over the place. One might think of being humiliated.

The man picked himself up. And with a smile on his face he spoke out loudly, "Finally, I have fallen into the right place!"

He was hired the very next moment.

A negative happening also can be converted into positive, if we develop the right attitude.

Humanity

A nurse took the tired, anxious serviceman to the bedside. "Your son is here," she said to the old man. She had to repeat the words several times before the patient's eyes opened. Heavily sedated because of the pain of his heart attack, he vaguely saw the young uniformed marine standing alongside. He reached out his hand. The marine wrapped his toughened fingers around the old man's limp ones, squeezing a message of love and encouragement.

The nurse brought a chair so that the marine could sit beside the bed. All through the night the young marine sat there in the poorly lit ward, holding the old man's hand and offering him words of love and strength. Occasionally, the nurse suggested that the marine move away and rest a while. He refused.

Whenever the nurse came into the ward, she noticed that the marine was oblivious of his surroundings. The oxygen tank clanked. Staff members laughed and exchanged greetings. Other patients cried and moaned. He was completely focussed on the patient and now and then she heard him say a few gentle words to him. The dying man remained silent, clutching the marine's hand throughout the night.

Towards dawn, the old man died. The marine released the now lifeless hand he had been holding and went to tell the nurse. While she did what she had to do, he waited. Finally, she returned. She started to offer words of sympathy, but the marine interrupted her. "Who was that man?" he asked. The nurse was startled, "He was your father," she answered. "No, he wasn't," the marine replied. "I never saw him before in my life."

"Then why didn't you say something when I took you to him?"

"I knew right away there had been a mistake, but I also knew he needed his son, and his son just wasn't there. When I realised that he was too sick to tell whether or not I was his son, knowing how much he needed me, I stayed."

Finding the Gaps

Ricky Ponting scored more than 27,000 runs in Test Cricket and ODIs.

When it comes to 'finding the gaps' Ricky Ponting is acknowledged as the Complete Master.

When asked about his ability to find so many gaps, Ponting replied, "Every Batsman assesses the field before taking strike, and usually the fielders' positions get imprinted on his mind. He can see every fielder in his mind's eye. But in my head, I don't see the fielders. I see only the gaps."

Our life in many ways is like the game of cricket. We should focus on Opportunities and not on Obstacles.

Martina Navratilova was once asked, "How do you maintain your focus, physique and sharp game even at the age of 43?"

She gave a humble reply, "The ball doesn't know how old I am."

We need to stop ourselves from stopping ourselves. Every game in life is actually played on a 6 inch stretch—the space between our two ears.

We don't live in bungalows, duplexes or flats. We live in our mind, which is an unlimited area. Life is great when things are sorted and uncluttered there.

The key factor to performing well in life and in every arena is the ability to control the quality and quantity of our 'internal dialogue'.

Taxing the Rich

In 1888, in Curacao a bridge was built to connect two parts of the city. A toll tax was proposed but officials wanted it to be a 'progressive' tax. They decided rich people will pay more to cross. So how to identify rich and poor quickly?

They had an idea, rich people wore shoes (it was 1888 remember), so they decided to charge a tax based on that. If you cross the bridge wearing shoes, you pay a tax, but if you are barefoot, you cross for free.

Simple, easy, difficult to avoid, a brilliant idea.

But it failed.

Why?

The rich simply took off their shoes and crossed the bridge in order to avoid tax.

The poor?

They did not want to be seen as poor, so they would wear shoes or borrow shoes to cross the bridge.

This is a true story.

So what are the lessons?

1. Rich stay rich by spending less.
2. Poor stay poor by spending more.
3. Rich always get better financial advice.
4. Taxing the rich to help the poor sounds great but it is complicated.

Ask yourself.....

Are you 'borrowing shoes' to cross any 'bridge?'

If you are, please stop.

More than 130 years have passed. This lesson holds true now too.

The Best Defence

When ancient Chinese decided to live in peace, they made the Great Wall of China. They thought no one could climb it due to its height. During the first 100 years of its existence, the Chinese were invaded thrice. Every time, the hordes of enemy infantry had no need of penetrating or climbing over the wall, because each time, they bribed the guards and came through the doors.

The Chinese built the wall but forgot the character-building of the wall-guards. They realised much later that the best defence against the enemy is not a fortified wall, but a fortified character. Thus, building of human character comes before building of anything else.

As Billy Graham once said, "When wealth is lost, nothing is lost; when health is lost, something is lost; when character is lost, all is lost."

The most selfish 1 letter word is ***I****, avoid it.*

The most satisfying 2-letter word is ***WE****, trust it.*

The most poisonous 3-letter word is ***EGO****, kill it.*

The most used 4-letter word is ***LOVE****, value it.*

The most pleasing 5-letter word is ***SMILE****, keep it.*

The fastest spreading 6-letter word is ***RUMOUR****, ignore it.*

The hardest working 7-letter word is ***SUCCESS****, achieve it.*

The most enviable 8-letter word is ***JEALOUSY****, distance it.*

The most powerful 9-letter word is ***KNOWLEDGE****, acquire it.*

The most essential 10-letter word is ***CONFIDENCE****, use it.*

The Sun and the Cave

There is a beautiful Sufi Story. One day the sun and a cave struck up a conversation. The sun had trouble understanding what 'dark' meant and the cave didn't quite get the hang of 'light and clear', so they decided to visit each other.

The cave went up to the sun and said, "Ah, I see, this is beyond wonderful. Now come down and see where I have been living."

The sun went down to the cave and said, "Gee, I don't see any difference."

When the sun went down, it took its light along and even the darkest corners were illuminated. That's why the sun couldn't see any difference.

If you are full of darkness, full of negativity, fear and doubt, you unknowingly become a cave. It's a hell within and no matter how much you accumulate, you still remain hollow.

On the other hand, if you are illuminated like the sun, then the darkness of the cave wouldn't matter. You could be in the worst of circumstances, yet you will still be able to find a blessing somewhere.

The enlightened ones can never be sent to hell or pushed into darkness. They carry their heaven on their shoulders all the time.

"Who will work in my absence?" Sun asked during sunset.

Everyone remained silent.

The Candle whispered, "I will try my level best."

It's not the matter of size or status, it's the attitude that shines.

Oldies Wisdom

Two old ladies Dolly and Meena were talking about their grandchildren.

Dolly said, "Every year I send each of my grandchildren a card with a generous cheque inside. I never hear from them nor receive a thank-you message."

Meena replied, "I too send them very generous cheques. I hear from them within a week after they receive it. In fact, they each pay me a personal visit."

"Wow! How come?" asked Dolly.

"Very simple solution. I don't sign the bloody cheque."

Husband to Wife: You should learn to embrace your mistakes.

She hugged him tightly.

* * *

Mrs. Das divorced Mr. Das.

Now she's bin-das.

* * *

An archeologist is the best husband any woman can have;

The older she gets, the more interested he is in her.

* * *

Don't worry about old age.

It doesn't last that long!

* * *

Don't marry the person you think you can live with. Marry the person you can't live without.

The Last Salute

My lead flight attendant came to me and said, "We have an H.R. on this flight." (H.R. stands for human remains.)

"Are they military?" I asked.

"Yes", she replied.

We completed our pre-flight checks, pushed back and performed an uneventful departure. About 30 minutes into our flight I received a call from the lead flight attendant in the cabin. "I just found out that the family of the soldier we are carrying, is on board", she said. She then proceeded to tell me that the father, mother, wife and 2-year old daughter were escorting their son, husband, and father home. The family was upset because they were unable to see the container that the soldier was in before we left. We were on our way to a major hub at which the family was going to wait for four hours for the connecting flight home.

The father of the soldier told the flight attendant that knowing his son was below him in the cargo compartment and being unable to see him was too much for him and the family to bear. He had asked the flight attendant if there was anything that could be done to allow them to see him upon our arrival. The family wanted to be outside by the cargo door to watch the soldier being taken off the airplane. I could hear the desperation in the flight attendant's voice when she asked me if there was anything I could do. "I'm on it", I said. I told her that I would get back to her.

Airborne communication with my company normally occurs in the form of e-mail messages. I decided to bypass this system and contacted my flight dispatcher directly on the phone. I explained the situation I had on board with the family, and what it was the family wanted. He said he understood and that he would get back to me.

Two hours went by and I had not heard from the dispatcher. We were going to get busy soon and I needed to know what to tell the family. I sent a text message asking for an update. I saved the return message from the dispatcher and the following is the text:

"Captain, sorry it has taken so long to get back to you. There is a policy on this now and I had to check on a few things. Upon your arrival a dedicated escort team will meet the aircraft. A van will be used to load the remains with a secondary van for the family. The family will be taken to their departure area and escorted into the terminal where the remains can be seen. It is a private area for the family only. When the connecting aircraft arrives, the family will be escorted to the plane side to watch the remains being loaded for the final leg home. Captain, most of us here in flight control are veterans. Please pass our condolences to the family. Thanks."

I sent a message back thanking flight control for a good job. I printed out the message and gave it to the lead flight attendant to pass on to the father. The lead flight attendant was very thankful and told me, "You have no idea how much this will mean to them."

Things started getting busy for the descent, approach and landing. After landing, we cleared the runway and taxied to the designated area. When we reached and checked in with the controller, we were informed that all traffic was being held for us, and a team was in place to meet us.

It looked like it was all coming together. Then I realised that once we turned the seat belt sign off, everyone would stand up at once and delay the family from getting off the airplane. As we approached our gate, I asked the co-pilot to tell the controller we were going to stop short of the gate to make an announcement to the passengers. He did that and the controller said, "Take your time."

I stopped the aircraft and set the parking brake. I pushed the public address button and said, "Ladies and gentleman, this is your Captain speaking. I have stopped short of our gate to make a special announcement. We have a passenger on board who deserves our honour and respect. His Name is Private Arun, a soldier who made the ultimate sacrifice. Private Arun is under your feet in the cargo hold. Escorting him today is Army Sergeant Gaurav. Also, on board are his father, mother, wife and daughter. We kindly request all passengers to remain in their seats to allow the family to exit the aircraft first. Thank you."

We continued towards the gate, came to a stop and started our shutdown procedures. A couple of minutes later I opened the cockpit door. I found the two forward flight attendants crying, something you just do not see. I was told that after we came to a stop, all passengers on the aircraft stayed in their seats, waiting for the family to exit the aircraft.

When the family got up and gathered their things, a passenger slowly started to clap his hands. Moments later more passengers joined in and soon the entire aircraft was clapping. Words of God bless you, I'm sorry, thank you, we are proud, and other kind words were uttered to the family as they made their way down the aisle and out of the airplane.

They were escorted down to finally be with their loved one. Many of the passengers disembarking thanked me for the announcement I had made. "They were just words", I told them, "I could say them over and over again, but nothing I say will bring back that brave soldier."

Please reflect on this event and the sacrifices that millions of our men and women have made to ensure our freedom and safety. We sleep peacefully, because they stand guard; we smile freely, because of their sacrifice.

Bus Ride to Remember

A few years ago, I was stuck on a bus in Delhi during rush hour. Traffic was barely moving. The bus was filled with cold, tired people who were deeply irritated with one another, and with the world itself. Two men barked at each other about a shove that might or might not have been intentional. A pregnant woman got on, and nobody offered her a seat. Rage was in the air, no mercy would be found here.

As the bus approached a stop, the driver got on the intercom. "Folks," he said, "I know you have had a rough day and you are frustrated. I can't do anything about the weather or traffic, but here is what I can do. As each one of you gets off the bus, I will reach out my hand to you. As you walk by, drop your troubles into the palm of my hand, okay? Don't take your problems home to your families tonight, just leave them with me. My route goes right by the Yamuna river, and when I drive by there later, I will open the window and throw your troubles in the water."

It was as if a spell had lifted. Everyone burst out laughing. Faces gleamed with surprised delight. People who had been pretending for the past hour not to notice each other's existence were suddenly grinning at each other like, is this guy serious?

Oh, he was serious!

At the next stop, just as promised, the driver reached out his hand, palm up, and waited. One by one, all the exiting commuters placed their hand just above his and mimed the gesture of dropping their troubles into his palm.

Some people laughed as they did this, some teared up, but everyone did it. The driver repeated the same lovely ritual at the next stop, too. And the next. All the way to the river.

Happiness is contagious. Start an epidemic today.

Friends

When silence is better than conversation
When understanding conquers separation
When poor knowledge of mathematics
Does not affect the interpersonal equation

When difference in thoughts does not matter
When similarity, dissimilarity does not matter
Gender, age, colour, creed also does not matter
When you can hold hands even over phone

When you are cherished for who you are
When it does not matter what you are not
When you don't have to measure your words
When you are not measured by your deeds

When wasting time together is fun
When being foolish together 'is in'
When lying on grass is time well spent
When facing a storm, oneness gives strength

When a mischievous grin brings sunshine
When a happy smile evaporates your pain
When a pat on head and a kick on backside is same
You are definitely with the best of friends!

With a dream in your pocket
And a smile on your face
Somehow this old world
Looks a much better place.

Die Empty

Die Empty by Todd Henry is one of the most thought provoking books to read. The author was inspired and got the idea of writing this book while attending a Business Meeting.

A speaker asked the audience, "Where is the richest land in the world?" One of the audience answered: "Oil-rich Gulf states." Another added: "Diamond mines in Africa."

The speaker said, "No, it is the cemetery. Yes, it is the richest land in the world. Millions of people have departed, and they carried many valuable ideas that did not come to light and could not benefit others. It is all in the cemetery where they are buried."

Inspired by this answer, Todd Henry wrote his book 'Die Empty'. The book motivates people to pour out their ideas and turn them into something useful before it is too late.

The most beautiful of what he said in the book is, "Do not go to your grave and carry inside you the best that you have. Always choose to Die Empty."

The true meaning of this expression is to die empty of all the valuable knowledge that is within you. Deliver it to the world, before you leave.

If you have an idea perform it.

If you have some special knowledge, give it out.

If you have a goal, achieve it.

Love, share and distribute, do not keep it inside.

Die Empty.

If you have knowledge, let others light their candles in it.

Team Work

A man was lost while driving through the countryside. As he tried to reach for the map, he accidentally drove off the road into a ditch. Though he wasn't injured, his car was stuck deep in the mud. So the man walked to a nearby farm to ask for help.

"Badal can get you out of that ditch," said the farmer, pointing to a horse standing in a field.

The man looked at the horse and looked at the farmer who just stood there repeating, "Yes, old Badal can do the job."

The man figured he had nothing to lose. The two men and the horse made their way back to the ditch. The farmer hitched the horse to the car. With a snap of the reins, he shouted, "Pull, Bhola! Pull, Moti! Pull, Hira! Pull, Badal!"

And Badal pulled that car right out of the ditch. The man was amazed. He thanked the farmer, patted the horse, and asked, "Why did you call out all those names before you called Badal?"

The farmer grinned and said, "Old Badal is blind. As long as he believes he's part of a team, he doesn't mind pulling."

A professor gave a balloon to every student, who had to inflate it, write their name on it and throw it in the hallway. The professor then mixed all the balloons. The students were given 10 minutes to find their own balloon. Despite a hectic search, most of them could not find their balloon. At that point the professor told the students to take the first balloon that they pick and hand it to the person whose name was written on it. Within 5 minutes everyone had their own balloon.

Flexible

An old lady handed her cheque to a bank cashier of a foreign bank and said, "I would like to withdraw Rs 2000." The cashier told her, "For withdrawals of less than Rs 5000, please use the ATM."

The lady then asked, "Why?"

The cashier irritably told her, "These are rules. Please leave if there is no other matter. There is a queue behind you." He then returned the cheque to her. The lady remained silent. But she returned the cheque to the cashier and said, "Please help me withdraw all the money I have."

The cashier was astonished when he checked the account balance. He nodded his head, leaned down and said to the old lady, "My apologies Granny, you have Rs 65 lakh in your account and our branch does not have so much cash currently. Could you make an appointment and come again tomorrow?"

The old lady then asked, "How much can I withdraw now?"

The cashier told her, "Any amount up to Rs 30,00,000."

The lady then told the cashier that she wanted to withdraw Rs 30,00,000 from her account. The cashier did so after much effort and handed it to her. The lady kept Rs 2000 in her bag and asked the cashier to deposit the balance amount back into her account. The cashier was dumbfounded.

The moral of the story is that rules are inflexible but we humans can be flexible when the situation requires us to be.

Attitude is a little thing that makes a big difference!

* * *

It takes considerable knowledge just to realise the extent of our own ignorance.

Two Kinds of Teachers

In Ramayana, Ram is educated by two teachers—Vashishtha and Vishwamitra. And these two teachers are as different from each other as day and night. Vashishtha is one of the primal seven sages. He is associated with Vedic wisdom. After Ram completes his studies, he travels around the world and returns disillusioned by the illusory nature of the world, uninterested in worldly life. Alarmed, his father Dasharatha seeks advice from Vashishtha who declares that this is a good thing, for Ram is now ready to receive the ultimate wisdom of the Vedas. Then follows, for 21 days, narration by Vashishtha in the king's court, after which an enlightened Ram is at peace with worldly life having understood the true meaning of life.

One of the lessons he learns is not to mistake correlation with causality. Just because a coconut falls from a tree when a crow alights on it does not mean the crow is the cause and the falling of the fruit is the effect. We often mistake events that may be coincidence to be causality and this is the cause of much sorrow in the world. Another lesson he learns is how in turbulent waters the moon has many reflections just as in turbulent minds we see many versions of reality and not the truth.

Vishwamitra, however, is a very different kind of teacher. Born a king, he was a great warrior before he decided to become a sage. He takes Ram into forest, ignoring Dasharatha's protests. There he makes Ram kill demon *Tadaka*, who used to disturb his yagna. He then makes Ram bring back to life Ahilya, wife of Rishi Gautama, who had been turned into stone on charge of adultery. Thus he makes Ram take life in one instance and give life in another. He takes Ram to Mithila where Ram strings the bow of Shiva and wins the hand of Janak's daughter Sita in marriage. With Vishwamitra, Ram does worldly things—killing, rescuing, learning about his lineage and securing a wife who will help him keep alive his family tree. These are worldly concerns.

Vashishtha comes across as spiritual while Vishwamitra comes across as material. Vashishtha brings a wider perspective to Ram while Vishwamitra brings an immediate focus. Both are valid.

The same idea is presented in a different way in Mahabharata. Under Drona, the Pandavas receive education that lets them fight wars and vanquish enemies. But only through Krishna do they gain spiritual wisdom—Vedic wisdom that explains the world to them, enabling Arjun to step out of despair and dilemma.

When you think about it, it is rather amazing that in both Ramayana and Mahabharata, Vedic wisdom or spiritual wisdom enables the protagonist to participate in worldly life. This wisdom does not make hermits of men, rather helps them transform into kings and warriors. Without this knowledge, there is disillusionment. The lessons of Vishwamitra and Drona may be practical and goal-driven but not enough to make us cope with moral and ethical issues that life brings our way.

There are two kinds of teachers in the corporate world. There are teachers at Business School who enable aspiring management students to think structurally about strategy, tactics, goals, objectives, planning, resource allocation, command and control. They guide students to review processes, go through balance sheets, negotiations and conflict resolution. They help the mind to think rationally and methodically to approach and solve a problem. These Vashishthas reappear in the corporate world as hard and soft skill trainers. These trainers help in learning, and facilitate to think about the work theoretically. They compel people to look at the subject in its purity, without the demands of practicality.

Then in the workplace, they meet their Vishwamitras, the mentors and coaches, who help them function well at the work place, give their best in practical situations. Many of these are bosses, who turn their subordinates into apprentices, teaching them how to deal with real life situations—from hiring to firing people, from negotiating with vendors to presenting before senior management. As one moves higher on the corporate ladder, the nature of the Guru changes. It becomes less about job at hand and processes and policies to be negotiated, and more about governance and managing people—preparing to be a leader.

We need both kinds of teachers in the corporate world. The theoretical and the practical, the spiritual and the material, the one who grants perspective and the one who helps with focus, in order to be successful in our corporate careers.

Do you appreciate the relevance of scriptures in modern education and all walks of life!

> *We all know the story of Eklavya. When Dronacharya asked him for his right thumb as Guru Dakshina, he unhesitatingly cut off the thumb and gave it to Dronacharya.*
>
> *There is a little known sequel to this story. Eklavya was asked whether he ever regretted the act of giving away his thumb. He replied, and the reply has to be believed to be true, as it was asked to him when he was dying.*
>
> *His reply was "Yes! I regretted this only once in my life. It was when Pandavas were coming in to kill Dronacharya, who was broken hearted on the false news of death of his son, Ashwathama, and had stopped fighting. It was then that I regretted the loss of my thumb. If the thumb was there, no one could have dared hurt my Guru."*

The Fresh Fish

The Japanese have always loved fresh fish. But the waters close to Japan do not have much fish for decades. So to feed the Japanese population, fishing boats got bigger and went farther than ever. The farther the fishermen went, the longer it took to bring in the fish. If the return trip took more than a few days, the fish did not remain fresh. The Japanese did not like the taste.

To solve this problem, fishing companies installed freezers on their boats. They would catch the fish and freeze them at sea. Freezers allowed the boats to go farther and stay longer. However, the Japanese could taste the difference between fresh and frozen and they did not like frozen fish. The frozen fish brought a lower price. So fishing companies installed fish tanks. They would catch the fish and stuff them in the tanks, fin to fin. After a little thrashing around, the fish stopped moving. They were tired and dull, but alive. Unfortunately, the Japanese could still taste the difference. Because the fish did not move for days, they lost their fresh-fish taste. The Japanese preferred the lively taste of fresh fish, not sluggish fish.

Here is how the Japanese solved this problem. To keep the fish tasting fresh, the Japanese fishing companies still put the fish in the tanks. But now they add a small shark to each tank. The shark eats a few fish, but most of the fish arrive in a very lively state. The fish are challenged!

Similarly, many of us sometimes feel stagnant and uninspired, like fish in a pond. So we need a shark in our life to keep us awake and moving. Basically in our lives sharks are new challenges to keep us active and lively.

Challenges are the heartbeat of growth. Embrace challenges, for they sculpt the strongest version of ourselves.

To the Child in Me

They told me to behave maturely,
so I forgot how to be naughty.

They told me not to be naive,
so I forgot how to be innocent.

They told me not to trust easily,
so I forgot to have faith.

They told me life is unfair,
so I forgot how to be fair.

They told me that this is a fake world,
so I forgot how to be genuine.

They told me bigger is better,
so I forgot the little things that made me smile.

They told me money is the prime source of happiness,
so I focused on earning money and forgot how to be happy.

They told me everything comes with a tag 'conditions apply',
so I forgot how to love unconditionally.

They told me you're an adult now,
so I forgot how to be a child.

Being on spiritual path means understanding that the source of your trouble and source of your well-being are within you.

* * *

The greatest challenge in life is discovering who you are.

The second greatest is being happy with what you find!

Untying Mental Blocks

A farmer was taking three of his donkeys for sale to the market. Along the way, he came across a river and decided to have a dip. Since he had only two ropes to tie the donkeys to a tree, he looked around wondering how to tie the third one.

He approached a sage nearby and asked if he could lend him a rope to tie the third donkey. The sage did not have a rope but offered a clever suggestion. He told the farmer, "Let the third donkey see you tying the other two donkeys to a tree. Then you pretend to tie this one also." The farmer did as he was told and went for a dip in the river.

Upon returning, he thanked the sage and found that the donkeys stood exactly at the same spot where he had left them. He untied the two donkeys and patted the third one to start moving. After going a little distance, he realised that the third donkey still stood at the same spot. Cajoling, kicking or talking did not help, with the donkey refusing to move from the spot.

The farmer went back to the sage, who told him, "Untie the third donkey".

"But", protested the farmer, "I have not tied him".

The sage replied, "You know it. But does the donkey know that?"

Sure enough the farmer went through the motions of untying the donkey. The donkey moved immediately as though released and walked over to join the other two donkeys.

We too are tied up by too many imaginary ropes which are really non-existent. The only truth is that there are no boundaries in real life and anyone can stretch to any extent.

> *It can be said with certainty that mind is the most valued real estate.*

Has the Water Entered My Ship

There are many of us who are so engrossed in our professional lives that we neglect our family and social responsibilities. If asked why we do this, we would reply that "We are doing it for our family."

Yet, our kids are sleeping when we leave home. They are sleeping when we come back home! Twenty years later, we'll turn back, and they'll all be gone, to pursue their own dreams and their own lives.

Without water, a ship cannot move. The ship needs water, but if the water gets into the ship, the ship will face existential problems. What was once a means of living for the ship will now become a means of destruction.

Similarly we live in a time where earning is a necessity but let not the earning enter our hearts, for what was once a means of living will surely become a means of destruction for us as well.

So take a moment and ask yourself, "Has the water entered my ship?" I hope not!

One day our entire life will be like a movie in a flash back. We just need to make sure that it is worth watching!

* * *

So many things I don't possess
Alas, how poor am I
And yet, so much of worth I have
The hills, the trees, the sky
The love of friends, my home, my health
I simply can not count my wealth!

Shoe Maker

On his first day in office, as President Abraham Lincoln entered to give his inaugural address, one man stood up. He was a rich Aristocrat. He Said, "Mr. Lincoln, you should not forget that your father used to make shoes for my family."

And the whole Senate laughed. They thought they had made a fool of Lincoln. But certain people are made of a totally different mettle. Lincoln looked at the man directly in the eyes and said, "Sir, I know that my father used to make shoes for your family, and there will be many others here, because he made shoes the way nobody else can. He was a creator. His shoes were not just shoes. He poured his whole soul into them. I want to ask you, have you any complain? Because I know how to make shoes myself. If you have any complain, I can make you another pair of shoes. But as far as I know, nobody has ever complained about my father's shoes. He was a genius, a great creator, and I am proud of my father."

The whole Senate was dumbstruck. They could not understand what kind of a man Abraham Lincoln was. He was proud because his father did his job so well that not even a single complain had ever been heard.

Remember, no one can hurt us without our consent. It is not what happens to us that hurts us. It is our response that hurts us.

> *Elitists never tire of repeating that only the chosen few matter; the majority are pigs. Yet it does happen that a he pig marries a she pig, and a Leonardo da Vinci is born.*
>
> * * *
>
> *Here are two sides of the same mystical coin—No one on earth can do you good except you yourself; no one can harm you except you yourself.*

Clever Deal

A ship was returning to its native land. Suddenly the ocean became wild... great winds, and the ship was almost on the verge of sinking. Everybody started praying. At such a moment who will not pray? Even the atheist will pray, the agnostic will pray, "Forgive me for what I have been saying, it was all nonsense. Forgive me, but let me reach the shore."

There was a Sufi on the ship, simply sitting there, not praying. People became annoyed and said, "You are a religious man, wearing the green robe of a Sufi. What kind of a Sufi are you? You should have been the first to pray. And we are not religious people, we are just business people, and to us this prayer is nothing but business. We are offering God, "We will give you this, we will give you that, just save us. Why are you sitting silently? Why are you not praying?"

The Sufi said, "I am not a businessman. If he wants to finish us all, good. If he wants to save us, good. I am in total agreement with him. Why should I pray? For what? Prayer means some disagreement, something is happening which you don't want to happen. You want God to intercede, to interfere, to stop it, to change it."

The Sufi continued, "I have no business of my own. It is his business to bother whether to save or to drown us. If he wants me to be saved, it is his business, not my business. And if he wants me to die, that is his business. I had not asked him for birth; suddenly I was here. I cannot ask him about death. If birth is not in my control, how can death be in my control?"

Those people thought, "This man is mad." They said, "We will take care of you later. Let us get to the shore somehow and then we will take care of you. You are not a Sufi, you are not religious; you are a very dangerous man. But this is not the time to bother and quarrel with you."

On board was a wealthy, famous man of the country, and he was coming with a huge amount of diamonds and precious stones. He had earned much. He had a beautiful palace in town—the most beautiful marble palace. Even the king was jealous. The king had asked him many times, "You give this palace to me—any price, and I will pay for it." But the rich man had always declined, "That is not possible. That palace is my pride."

When the ship was almost sinking, the man shouted to God, "Listen, I will give that palace to you—just save me!" And as it happened, the winds disappeared, the ocean became calm, the ship was saved. They reached the shore.

Now the rich man was in a very difficult situation because of what he had said. And he had been angry with the Sufi—now he was not angry. He said, "Perhaps you were right to keep quiet. If I had followed you, I would not have lost my palace. But I am a businessman, and I will find a way." And he found a way.

Next day he put the palace up for auction. He informed all the nearby kingdoms. Many kings, queens and rich people came; everybody was interested. There was a cat chained to a marble pillar of the palace. The rich man came out and said, "This palace and the cat, both are up for auction together as a package. The price of the cat is one million dinars and the price of the palace, one dinar; total one million and one dinar."

People said, "For this cat one million dinar, and for this palace just one dinar?" The businessman said, "You don't bother about it. If you are interested, both are going to be sold together. If anybody is interested, this is my minimum price." The king of the country said, "I will give you the price, but please tell me, what is the secret of this cat and the palace?"

The businessman said, "No secret, I just got into trouble because of a prayer. I have told God that 'I will give you the palace.' And I am a businessman; if he is a businessman, I am also a businessman. The cat is for one million dinars—that I will keep. The palace is for one dinar—that I will give towards God's fund."

Tongue

Strolling through the streets of Lanka at night, Hanuman was taken aback when he heard the soft chants of *Sriram* from the window of a house. Hanuman wondered who could be chanting the Lord's name in a city ruled by Ravan. The house had a cluster of *Tulsi* plants outside and the walls had signs of *Sri Hari*.

Just then a man opened the front door and came out chanting the holy name. The sky was starlit, dawn was still a couple of hours away. The man offered water to the *Tulsi* plants, while circumbulating.

As Hanuman appeared before him, with folded hands, the man introduced himself as Vibhishana, brother of Ravan. Hanuman asked, "It baffles me, you're such a devotee and a noble soul. How on earth do you live among the demons?"

Vibhishana smiled and said, "Just as the tongue lives in the mouth. With 32 teeth biting and grinding around it, not only does the tongue remain untouched, it enjoys all the flavours. The very food that sits and rolls on the tongue is chewed to a pulp by the teeth and yet this little thing escapes unscathed! The only time it is hurt is when we have a lapse of mindfulness."

The tongue teaches us that others may grind and bite but we can still enjoy life if we are flexible. Everything will hurt less, bother less if we loosen up a bit. Speaking sweetly and respectfully releases waves of sweetness and joy. The world around cares for truth but it cares a lot more about how you tell the truth. If you want lasting peace and joy learn from your tongue and live like it. Befriend it, tame it. It has a great bearing on your relationships.

If your eyes are positive, you will like the world.

If your tongue is positive, the world will like you.

Sometimes

Sometimes,
I feel I want to go back in time...
Not to change things, but to feel a couple of things again.

Sometimes,
I wish I was a baby for a while...
Not to be walked in the pram but to see my mother's smile.

Sometimes,
I wish I could go back to school...
Not to become a child but to spend more time with those friends,
I never met after school.

Sometimes,
I wish I could be back in college...
Not to be a rebel but to really understand what I studied.

Sometimes,
I wish I was a fresher at my work...
Not to do less work but to recall the joy of the first pay cheque.

Sometimes,
I wish my kids were younger...
Not because they grew fast but to play with them a bit more.

Sometimes,
I feel I still had some more time to live...
Not to have a longer life but to know what I could give to others.

Sometimes, you find yourself in the middle of nowhere.
And sometimes, in the middle of nowhere, you find yourself.

Father and Son

When I came to Mumbai, I stayed as a paying guest in a posh building in Pali Hill. Not that I could afford it, but I was lucky to get it cheap for an emotional reason. The landlords were an old couple and the apartment was huge. Their children were all abroad. They were lonely and afraid that if something happens to them who would be there to take them to hospital.

They gave me a small room to live. I was struggling and used to buy very cheap food like bhelpuri, vada pao, etc. from Linking Road, warm it in their microwave and eat alone in my room.

One day, auntie asked me to eat in their dining room. So next day, I bought some extra bhelpuri and offered them. Hesitantly, they accepted it. Uncle told me that it was after some 20 years they had eaten street food, as their children had stopped them from eating street food.

Slowly, this became a ritual. They started waiting for me to come back with some street food. This brought joy in their life. It also gave me a sense of family. They told me this must remain a 'secret' between us and I must never tell their children, just in case we ever met. Their children called every weekend but they never ever mentioned this 'secret'.

I started finding out all famous street food vendors in Mumbai. I travelled in local trains, walked miles to get some special street food from corners of Mumbai. *Kheema Pav* of Gulshan-e-Iran at Crawford Market, *Dosa* from Anand at Ville Parle, *Bun Maska* and *Mava Samosa* of Mervan's at Grant Road, *Samosa* with *Choley* of Guru Kripa in Sion, *Khichdi* of Swati Snacks, *Sadguru Pav Bhaji* from Chembur...

It gave me a purpose, and hope to old couple. We became a small family seeking that 'dining table' moment of bonding. Uncle was very old, 90ish. He would tell me the same tales every day.

Later, I learnt from auntie that the entire day he didn't speak. This was the only time when he came to life.

Gradually, his health started deteriorating. He started forgetting. Then came a time when he forgot that I wasn't his real son. One day, on his birthday, I brought *poori aloo ki sabzi* from Pancham Pooriwala near VT station. He smelt it for a very long time and then he called me by his son's name. Auntie told me most of his working life in town, he had same *poori aloo* for lunch as his office was next door to Pancham. Once he retired, his son told him not to eat it anymore. After relishing it for more than an hour, he got up and walked very slowly, with his walker, to his room and came back with a box. Once again, he addressed me by his son's name and gave it to me. "I had kept it for the day when you grow up to fulfill a son's duty. Today, you did it. It's yours now."

When I opened the box, there was a 'Hero' fountain pen in it. Later auntie told me that uncle had written his engineering exam with this. The pen was gifted to him by his father.

That night, I hadn't found a Hero pen. I had found a father. We are born to one father. But we can be son to many fathers.

That pen is with me to be given to a son who will bring me my favourite food, when I am old and cold.

> *An artist made a beautiful painting of heart. Then he drew a small door in it. But there was no handle in the door. Somebody asked the artist, why he had not made the handle. The artist replied, "the doors of the heart open from inside, not from outside".*
>
> * * *
>
> *Happiness is like a butterfly, which, when pursued, is always beyond our grasp, but, which, if you will sit down quietly, may alight upon you.*

Never Allow a Cat in Your Life

A great saint was dying and he said to his successor, a young man, "Remember one thing, never allow a cat in your life", and he died. A big crowd had gathered to listen to the last sermon of this great saint... and what a sermon!

"Never allow a cat in your life." The successor said, "My God, why should I allow a cat in my life in the first place?"

An old man—who was also a disciple, said, "You don't know, there is a long story behind it. He has just given you the punch line." The successor said, "Then I must know the whole story."

The story was that when the saint renounced his wife, children and home, and went into the Himalayas, he lived near a small village. The villagers were happy that they had a saint of their own, so they made a small bamboo hut for him.

The saint used to wear just a loincloth. Trouble arose when some rats came into the hut and started chewing the loincloth. The man was in great difficulty; he had only two loinclothes and soon they would be gone. So he asked the villagers, "What to do? My sect does not allow a saint to have more than two loinclothes. That's the only possession allowed."

The villagers said, "Why don't you take a cat from the village? She will kill the rats." It was a perfectly rational solution. So the villagers gave him a good cat, and the cat killed the rats. But the problem was, now he had to beg for his food and the cat also needed something to eat, because the rats were finished. So he had to beg for some milk for the cat.

The villagers said, "The whole village can contribute some money and purchase a cow, and in that way you will have enough milk for yourself and your cat."

It looked right, so a healthy cow was brought in. Now the problem was that the cow needed grass. So every day he had to go to the village to beg for grass. People said, "This does not look right. A great saint asking for grass. In fact no saint has ever asked for grass; it is not conventional."

He said, "But what to do? My cow, my cat..."

So they said, "A simple solution, we are villagers, we don't know much about your philosophy. One woman has become a widow; her husband has died, and she has nobody. So we will persuade her. She will be really happy to serve a saint and then you don't have to come every day. We will clear some ground by the side of your hut so she can grow grass, she can grow wheat... and she will take care of you in sickness."

The idea was right. It was not much effort to persuade the woman; she was alone and so she agreed. She started taking care of the saint, his cow, cat and kitchen. The saint and the woman started working in the field, growing wheat and grass. The cat was very happy and the cow was very happy, everything was perfect. But then the ultimate happened. The woman was beautiful, the saint was not very old. What more is needed? They started developing feelings for each other and the widow became pregnant. In due course the saint became father to a few children.

People started laughing at him, "What kind of saint are you? You are keeping a woman! You have fallen down from your greatness."

Then the saint thought, "Oh my God, what have I done! I had renounced the world—this is the whole world again! It grew so slowly that I was not aware until the children came."

Now, just because of the cat the whole world came in. The old disciple said, "That was the punch line. He told you, 'not to allow a cat', because behind the cat the whole world comes in. He was talking about his own life story, how he again became engaged in the same world."

A Tale of Two Seas

Sitting in the Geography class in school, I remember how fascinated I was when we were being taught about the Dead Sea. As you probably recall, the Dead Sea is really a lake, not a sea. It is so high in salt content that the human body can float easily. You can almost lie down and read a book! The salt in the Dead Sea is as high as 35%, almost 10 times the normal ocean water. And all that saltiness has meant that there is no life at all in the Dead Sea. No fish, no vegetation, no sea animals. Nothing lives in the Dead Sea. And hence the name—Dead Sea.

While the Dead Sea has remained etched in my memory, I don't seem to recall learning about the Sea of Galilee in my school Geography lesson. So when I heard about the Sea of Galilee and the Dead Sea and the tale of the two seas—I was intrigued. Turns out that the Sea of Galilee is just north of the Dead Sea. Both the Sea of Galilee and the Dead Sea receive their water from river Jordan. And yet, they are very, very different.

Unlike the Dead Sea, the Sea of Galilee is pretty resplendent with rich colourful marine life. There are lots of plants. And lots of fish too. In fact, the Sea of Galilee is home to over twenty different types of fish.

Same region, same source of water, and yet while one sea is full of life, the other is dead. How come?

Here apparently is why. River Jordan flows into the Sea of Galilee and then flows out. The water simply passes through the Sea of Galilee, in and then out, and that keeps the Sea healthy and vibrant, teeming with marine life.

But the Dead Sea is so far below the mean sea level, that it has no outlet. The water flows in from river Jordan, but does not flow out. There are no outlet streams. It is estimated that over a million tons of water evaporate from Dead Sea every day, leaving it salty. It is too full of minerals and unfit for any marine life.

The Dead Sea takes water from River Jordan, and holds it. It does not give. Result? No life at all. Think about it.

Life is not just about getting and acquiring. It is about giving and sharing. We all need to be a bit like the Sea of Galilee.

We are fortunate to have wealth, knowledge, love and respect. But if we do not learn to give, we could all end up like the Dead Sea. The love and respect, wealth, beauty and knowledge would all evaporate with time. Just like the water of Dead Sea.

If we get the Dead Sea mentality of merely taking in more goods, more money, more of everything, the result can be disastrous. It will be a good idea to make sure that in the sea of your own life, you must have outlets. Many outlets. For love and for wealth, and everything else that you get in your life. Make sure you don't just keep it to yourself, you must give it away too. Open the taps of your mind. And you'll open the floodgates to happiness.

The quickest way to lift our living level is to lift our giving level.

* * *

We make a living by what we get, but we make a life by what we give.

* * *

If a drop of water falls in a lake, its identity is lost.

But

If a drop of water falls on a lotus leaf, it shines like a pearl.

Drop is the same,

but the 'COMPANY' matters.

Caste of a Mother

He questioned her, "Which caste do you belong to?"

She asked back, "As a woman or as a mother?"

A bit perplexed, the man said, "Tell me about both."

With full confidence, she started telling...

"Till a woman becomes a mother, she belongs to the caste she is born into without her choice. But the day she becomes a mother, she becomes casteless!"

He was taken aback. "How is it possible?"

Her answer was...

"When a mother cleans excreta of her child, she belongs to *shoodra jati*.

As the child grows, she protects the child from harm and unwanted influences, she turns into a *kshatriya*.

When she imparts good *sanskars* or good values, good culture and education to her child, she becomes a *brahmin*.

And last but not the least,

When the child grows up further, the mother makes him worldly wise and guides him to financial stability, she becomes a *vaishya*.

So I hope you agree with my statement that a woman has no caste, she is casteless."

Listening to this, the man was dumbstruck. His eyes and demeanour reflected deep respect for her, and felt highly enlightened.

> *The moment a child is born, the mother is also born. She never existed before. The woman existed, but the mother, never.*

Soar Like an Eagle

An eagle can foresee when a storm is approaching, long before it breaks. Instead of hiding, the eagle flies to some high point and waits for the winds to come. When the storm hits, it sets its wings so that the wind can pick it up and lift it above the storm. While the storm rages below, the eagle soars above it.

The eagle does not escape or hide from the storm; instead, it uses the storm to lift it higher. It rises on the stormy winds which others dread.

When the storm of life or challenges hit us, we can rise above them and soar like the eagle that rides the storm's winds. Don't be afraid of the storms or the challenges in your life. Use it to lift yourself higher.

If you have a project idea and it is rejected two or three times, you will surely give in to despair and frustration. But it was different with Colonel Sanders. His idea was rejected more than 1000 times. When he was 65 years old, he found himself penniless. But he did not give up and kept at it until a restaurant agreed to use his recipe, which was called Kentucky Fried Chicken, and for every piece of chicken sold, he was given a small percentage.

He kept on collecting the money, and in 1952 opened the first branch of KFC, which was a great success. Today the number of KFC branches is more than 20,000 around the world!

* * *

Life is only froth and bubble

Two things stand like stone

Caring in another's trouble

Courage in your own.

Changing Vision

There once lived a wealthy man who was bothered by severe eye pain. He consulted many physicians, but none could treat his ache. He went through a myriad of treatment procedures, but his pain persisted with more vigour. He looked for every available solution for his pain and finally approached a wise monk renowned for treating various illnesses. The monk carefully observed the man's eyes and offered a very peculiar solution.

The monk told the man to concentrate only on green colour for a few weeks and avoid other colours. The man was desperate to get rid of the pain and was determined, ready to go to any extent. The wealthy man appointed a group of painters, purchased green paint barrels and directed that every object his eyes was likely to fall to be painted green.

After a few weeks, the monk came to visit the man to follow up on the man's progress. As the monk walked towards the man's room, the appointed painter poured a bucket of green paint on the monk. The monk could see that the whole corridor and the room were painted green. As the monk inquired about the reason for painting everything green, the wealthy man said that he was only following the monk's advice to look at only green.

Hearing this, the monk laughed and said, "If only you had purchased a pair of green spectacles worth just a small amount, you could have saved a large share of your fortune. You cannot paint the world green."

Moral: Let us change our vision, and the world will appear accordingly.

> *Do not grieve that rose plants have thorns, rather rejoice that thorny bushes have roses.*

Commitment

In Giza zoo, there was a tigress named Salha. Her husband, the male tiger, had chronic rheumatism that made him hard to move. So the zoo management decided to take him out of their love nest and bring another tiger to mate tigress Salha, so as to keep the breed of tigers growing.

When they brought the new tiger, the tigress revolted and attacked him, so they returned him to where he came from, and the tigress was left alone.

Whew, the tigress went on an indefinite fast in grief for her husband, the sick tiger they took away from her. She thought that he would not return to her, as either he had died of the disease or was shot dead, so she decided to die and follow him.

Because of her indefinite fast, the zoo management had to return her sick husband to her. She received him with great joy and licked him, then she peacefully slept next to him.

This loyal tigress preferred the companionship of her sick husband to watch over his comfort, take care of him, and nurse him rather than the companionship of a new healthy and strong groom.

This predator is kinder than many humans!

Kindness is a language the deaf can hear, the blind can see and the mute can speak.

* * *

Love is the only flower that grows and blossoms without the aid of seasons.

What is Wealth

A few years ago there was a conference in United States on investment and finance. One of the speakers was Elon Musk and during the question answer session, he was asked a question that had everyone laughing. *"Will he, the richest man in the world, accept that his daughter marries a poor or a modest man."*

His answer can change something in everyone. Elon Musk responded, "First of all, we should understand that wealth does not mean having a fat bank account. Wealth is primarily the ability to create wealth. For example, someone who wins a lottery or jackpot in gambling, even if he wins 100 millions, he is not a rich man. He is a poor man with a lots of money. That's the reason why 90% of lottery millionaires become poor again within 5 years.

You also have rich people who have no money, for example, most entrepreneurs. They are already on the road to wealth even though they have no money, because they are developing their financial intelligence and that is wealth.

If you see a young person who decides to learn new things, who tries to improve himself constantly, know that he is a rich man.

If you see a young person who thinks that the problem is the state, who thinks that the rich are all thieves and who criticises constantly, know that he is a poor man.

The rich are convinced that they just need information and training to take off, the poor think that others must give them money to take off.

In conclusion, when I say that my daughter will not marry a poor man, I am not talking about money. I'm talking about the ability to create wealth in that man.

Excuse me for saying this, but most criminals are poor people. When they are in front of money, they lose their mind, that's why they rob, steal etc. For them it is a grace because they don't know how they could earn money by themselves.

One day, the guard of a bank found a bag full of money. He took the bag and went to give it to the bank manager. People called this man an idiot, but in reality this man was just a rich man who had no money. One year later, the bank offered him a job as a receptionist, 3 years later he was a customer manager and 10 years later he manages the regional management of this bank, he manages hundreds of employees and his annual bonus exceeds the amount he could have stolen.

Wealth is afterall a state of mind!"

A poor man asked Buddha, "Why am I so poor?"

Buddha said, "Because you do not learn to give."

The poor man said, "But I'm not having anything?"

Buddha said: "You have a few things ...

—The Face, which can give a smile;

—The Mouth, which can praise or comfort others;

—The Heart, which can open up to others;

—The Eyes, which can admire others;

—The Body, which can be used to help others."

* * *

A young newly appointed company's manager made a deal, in which his company lost one million rupees. He came to the office, feeling his guilt and not waiting until the owner would tell him something, said: "I understand that you can sack me, and I, admitting my guilt, accept your decision."

"To sack you?" The owner said: "I have just spent one million on your training and may not throw such valuable human resource. Go to work!"

Patience

Zorba the Greek tells of his own lesson in patience: "I remember one morning when I discovered a cocoon in the bark of a tree. There a butterfly was making a hole in its case and preparing to come out. I waited a while but it was too long appearing and I was impatient.

I bent over it and breathed on it to warm it. I warmed it as quickly as I could and a miracle began to unfold before my eyes. The case opened, the butterfly started slowly crawling out. But I shall never forget my horror when I saw how its wings were folded back and crumpled. The wretched butterfly tried with all its trembling body to unfold them.

Bending over it, I tried to help it with my breath, but in vain. It needed to be hatched out patiently and the unfolding of the wings needed to be a gradual process in the sun. Now it was too late. My breath had forced the butterfly to appear, all crumpled, before its time. It struggled desperately, and a few seconds later, died in the palm of my hand."

If an egg is broken by an outside force ... a life ends.

If an egg breaks from within ... life begins.

Great things always begin from within.

* * *

A wise old owl sat on an oak,
The more he saw the less he spoke.
The less he spoke the more he heard,
Why are we not like that wise old bird?

Integrity

A German once visited a temple under construction where he saw a sculptor making an idol. He noticed a similar idol lying nearby. Surprised, he asked the sculptor, "Do you need two statues of the same idol?"

"No," said the sculptor without looking up, "We need only one, but the first one got damaged at the last stage."

The gentleman examined the idol and found no apparent damage. "Where is the damage?" He asked.

"There is a scratch on the nose of the idol." Said the sculptor, still busy with his work.

"Where are you going to install the idol?"

The sculptor replied that it would be installed on a pillar twenty feet high.

"If the idol is that far, who is going to know that there is a scratch on the nose?" The gentleman asked.

The sculptor stopped his work, looked up at the gentleman, smiled and said, "I will know it."

There is an Indian proverb or axiom that says that everyone is a house with four rooms:

- *physical*
- *mental*
- *emotional, and*
- *spiritual.*

Most of us tend to live in one room most of the time, but unless we go into every room every day, even if only to keep it aired, we are not a complete person.

The Art of Learning

There is a Chinese saying, 'You can't pour fresh hot tea into a cup of stale tea.' A renowned Professor went to a Zen master to know all about Zenism. After a few pleasantries and a little talk, the Master realised that the Professor was not open to fresh ideas. He invited the Professor for tea.

The Master started pouring tea and after a while it started overflowing the cup. The Professor shouted, "Master, no more will go in the cup."

The Master replied, "Yes, like this cup your mind is overflowing with your own ideas. You must empty your mind a little for new ideas to come in."

Well, unlock your mind—rather throw away the lock! Keep on using your mind so that more ideas can come in—fresh and new!

Before your Speak... Listen

Before you Write... Think

Before you Spend... Earn

Before you Hate... Love

Before you Quit... Try

Before you Die... Live.

* * *

I asked a monk how to feel tall.

He just smiled and bowed.

Bundle of Misery

A man used to pray the same prayer every night repeatedly asking, "Do this one favour to me—and I have been asking this my whole life. I am the most miserable person on earth. Why have you chosen me to be the most miserable? I am ready to exchange my misery with anybody else, anybody will do—just let me exchange my misery with somebody else. Can't you give me this single opportunity to exchange my misery with somebody else? This is not asking much!"

And one night in his dream a great voice comes saying, "Gather all your miseries into bundles and bring them to the temple hall." So the whole town gathers their miseries into big bundles and rush towards the temple. This man is tremendously happy. "The moment has come! It seems something is going to happen!" He rushes with his bundle. On the way he finds others also rushing. By the time he reaches the temple he becomes afraid, very afraid, because he sees people carrying much bigger bundles than his. People that he had always seen smiling, in beautiful clothes and big houses, partying all the time, they are carrying bigger bundles! He starts becoming a little hesitant whether to go or not to go. But he has been praying his whole life, so he says, "Let us see what happens." They enter the temple. The voice says, "Put down your bundle. Now you can replace it with any bundle that you like."

And the miracle of miracles happens. Everybody rushes to their own bundle! This man also rushes fast towards his own bundle, afraid that if somebody else chooses it then he will be at a loss. Everybody has chosen their own bundle, with great relief and they are all happy, carrying their bundles back to their homes. Even this man is very happy, for the simple reason that "who knows what is in the other's bundle? At least I am aware of my own bundle and what it contains. And I have become accustomed, I have become adjusted to my misery."

Renunciation

There is a beautiful story about Sant Kabir. Once a lady with her young child came to Sant Kabir and complained that her son had the habit of eating lot of Jaggery every day. Sant Kabir told her to come after a week.

Upon the lady's return after a week, Sant Kabir told the boy to give up the habit of eating Jaggery. The lady was surprised to hear this and asked Sant Kabir, "You could have said this when we had come earlier?"

Sant Kabir clarified to the lady, "How could I advise your son not to eat Jaggery when I used to eat it myself at that time? Therefore, these last seven days I practised to stay without eating Jaggery, so I could advise your son to do the same!"

The famous Turkish poet Nazim Hikmat requested his famous painter friend Abidin to make a painting on 'happiness'. So Abidin made a painting of a family of six sleeping peacefully on a creaking bed. One leg of that bed was broken and two bricks were placed there. The roof of that dilapidated house was leaking. The dog of the house was also sleeping peacefully on the bed. This painting of Abidin became immortal.

Think deeply about this immortal painting and discover what happiness really is! Actually, after seeing this painting, I feel that happiness is not the absence of problems, but in accepting the predicament with ease. Try to see the good in whatever you have, no matter how bad the situation is. Stop being sad about such things, which are not in your control. Whenever your heart starts sinking, look at this immortal painting of Abidin. Always be satisfied and sleep peacefully!

* * *

Life can be complicated, but Happiness is really simple.

Innovative Solution

In Kanpur Ordnance Factory's ammunition manufacturing unit, workers were required to wear special anti-static shoes. This was to prevent gun powder from being set off from static electricity when people walked around. These shoes were delicate and not designed to withstand everyday usage. Needless to say, the shoes were super costly too.

Nonetheless, workers still wore them outside the factory, walked on streets, rode bicycles etc. This withered off the shoes easily. The Ordnance factory was incurring a huge cost replacing these shoes.

Being a government factory, with the employees protected by unions, the management of the factory felt helpless in correcting the situation. In spite of repeated reminders, pleading and finally multiple warnings, there was no change in the behaviour of the workers.

A committee was set-up to come up with a solution. After much thought, one of the members suggested that the next order for the shoes should be like this—order all the right foot shoes in black and all the left foot shoes in white. No one will dare wear the contrasting pair of shoes outside in public.

Problem was solved. Compliance happened. Simply brilliant, isn't it?

> *No lock is manufactured without a key. Similarly, all problems have several solutions. To solve any problem, we have to delve a little higher in our intellect.*
>
> * * *
>
> *If we did all the things we are capable of doing, we would literally astonish ourselves.*

Where There's a Will, There's a Way

Samarth Mahangade was hard at work, his hands sticky with the juice of freshly pressed sugarcane as he served weekend travellers at his roadside stall on a crisp winter morning at Harrison's Folly, a stunning cliffside viewpoint, 5 km from Panchgani.

Then came the call. "Samarth, where are you? The exam's going to start soon. Late entry will not be allowed." It was his friend, his voice frantic. The 19-year-old BCom first-year student froze. The Natural Dissolution Management paper—his first-semester university exam that had been postponed—was today. And he had no clue because his hall ticket hadn't been updated. Panic set in.

The exam centre was in Pasarni village, at the base of the steep and winding Pasarni Ghat—15 km away. The serpentine road, notorious for its slow-moving traffic, would take at least 30 minutes—time he simply did not have.

His mind raced. He needed a miracle. And then it struck him—the sky. Across the clearing stood paragliding instructor Govind Yewale, who ran adventure flights from Harrison's Folly. Samarth sprinted toward him. "Bhau, I need your help. I have an exam in 10 minutes. Can you take me down there?"

Yewale frowned, his eyes narrowing. "An exam? And you forgot the date?" He shook his head, exasperated. But the urgency in the boy's eyes—it was impossible to ignore. After a moment's hesitation, Yewale waved over one of his paragliders. "Strap in," he ordered. "Hold on tight."

Heart pounding, Samarth was buckled into the harness. And then, with a running start, they leaped off the cliff. The ground fell away in an instant, and he was flying. In 5 minutes, they were over the exam centre.

As he soared through the sky, another friend rushed to his home, retrieving his hall ticket, writing pad and pen. The pilot expertly steered the glider, bringing them down onto the school ground. Samarth unbuckled himself mid-stride and ran. His lungs burned as he sprinted to the exam hall, bursting through the doors just as the question papers were being handed out.

A pause. Then, a nod. He was allowed in. He slid into his seat. Later, Samarth reflected on the whirlwind of the morning. "I work to support my family, but my education is just as important," he said.

Traffic congestion along Pasarni Ghat was common but not unusually severe that day. Still, it didn't matter. For one determined student, every second had counted.

Remember, when life throws you a curveball, take a leap of faith, just like Samarth did. You never know where it might take you.

When we have to go somewhere early in the morning, we set an alarm and go to sleep. However, sometimes even without an alarm, we wake up at the exact time we had planned. This is called Bio-Clock.

In Japan, many people believe they can live up to 120 years in good health. With this strong mental conviction, they have tuned their bio-clock accordingly.

Happiness and illness cannot coexist. Where there is one, the other cannot exist. So, stay happy to stay healthy. Every problem originates from our mind—our thought process, and especially our words. So, reset your mental 'bio-clock' for a longer lifespan. We must believe that there is no chance of diseases affecting us till we are 100.

Let us change our perspective, change our life so as to cherish life to the fullest!

Fair Value

This incident is about the famous jeweller Charles Tiffany and investment banker JP Morgan. One fine day, Tiffany found a diamond necktie pin, particularly uncommon and extraordinarily beautiful. He knew that Morgan had a liking for necktie pins. As was the custom those days, before 1900, he sent a messenger to Morgan's office with the pin fancily wrapped in a box and the following note, "Dear Mr. Morgan, knowing how much you appreciate necktie pins, I'm sending you this rare and exquisite piece for your consideration. Due to its rarity, the price is US $ 5,000. If you choose to accept it, please send a messenger to my office tomorrow with your cheque for US $ 5,000. If you choose not to accept it, you can send your messenger back with the pin."

The next day, Morgan's messenger arrived at Tiffany's with the same box in a new package and a different envelope. The envelope contained a note that read, "Dear Mr. Tiffany, the pin is really magnificent. However, US $ 5,000 is a little over the top. So, enclosed is a cheque for US $ 4,500. If you accept it, please send my messenger back with the box. If not, return the cheque and he will leave the box with you."

Tiffany looked at the cheque for several minutes as it was actually a lot of money. However, he was sure the pin was worth the US $ 5,000 he had asked for. Finally, he told the messenger, "You can return the cheque to Mr. Morgan. My price is firm." And thus, the messenger took the cheque back and put the gift-wrapped box on Tiffany's table. Tiffany sat down for a minute thinking about the cheque he had returned. Then he unwrapped the box to get the pin out.

Upon opening the box, he didn't find the pin but instead a cheque for US $ 5,000 from Morgan and a note with just one sentence: "Just Checking the Price."

Dirty Laundry

A young couple moved into a new neighbourhood. The next morning while they were having breakfast, the young woman saw her neighbour hanging the laundry outside. "The laundry is not very clean." She said. "She doesn't know how to wash properly, perhaps she needs better laundry soap."

Her husband looked on but remained silent. Every time her neighbour would hang her clothes to dry, the young woman would make the same comment.

About one month later, the woman was surprised to see a nice clean wash on the line and said to her husband: "Look, she has learned how to wash properly. I wonder who taught her this."

The husband said: "I got up early this morning and cleaned our windows."

And so it is with life. What we see when watching others depends on the purity of the window through which we look!!!

Trifles

A joke or a song or a handshake
A letter that comforts or cheers
A meeting or parting, more precious
Because of the smiles or tears
A five minutes sit after dinner
A 'thank you' that lends the heart wings
All these are but trifles, yet surely
They're also life's wonderful things!

Unaccomplished

Don't leave anything for later.

Later, the coffee gets cold.

Later, you lose interest.

Later, the day turns into night.

Later, life goes by.

Later, you regret not doing something when you had the chance.

Life is a fleeting dance, a delicate balance of moments that unfold before us, never to return in quite the same way again.

Regret is a bitter pill to swallow, a weight that bears down upon the soul with the burden of missed chances and unspoken words. So, let us not leave anything for later.

Let us seize the moments as they come, with open hearts and outstretched arms to embrace the possibilities that lie before us. For in the end, it is not the things we did that we regret, but the things we left undone, the words left unspoken, the dreams left unfulfilled.

Time is slow when you have to wait.

Time is fast when you are late.

Time is endless when you are in pain.

Time is short when you are happy.

Time is deadly when you are sad.

Time is long when you feel bored.

Everytime, time is determined by your feelings and your psychological conditions and not by clocks.

So have a nice time always!

Making a Difference

A man was walking down a deserted beach at sunset. As he walked along he began to see another man in the distance.

As he grew nearer he noticed that the local native kept leaning down, picking something up, and throwing it into the water. Time and again he kept hurling things into the ocean.

As our friend approached closer he noticed that the man was picking up starfish that had washed up onto the beach, and one at a time, he was throwing them back into the ocean.

The man was puzzled. He approached the native and said, "Good evening, friend, I was wondering what are you doing?" The native replied, "I'm throwing these starfish back into the ocean. You see, it's low tide right now and all these starfish have been washed up onto the shore. If I don't throw them back into the sea, they will die."

"I understand," the man replied "but there must be thousands of starfish on this beach and you couldn't possibly get to all of them. There are simply too many and don't you realize that this is happening on hundreds of beaches up and down this coast, can't you see that you can't possibly make a difference?"

The local native smiled, bent down, picked up yet another starfish, and as he threw it back out into the sea, he replied, "It made a difference to that one!"

We ourselves feel that what we are doing is just a drop in the ocean. But the ocean would be less because of that missing drop.

* * *

Extending one hand to help someone has more value than joining two hands in prayer!

Two Stories

Story Number One

Many years ago, Al Capone virtually owned Chicago. Capone wasn't famous for anything heroic. He was notorious for enmeshing the windy city in everything from bootlegged booze and prostitution to murder.

Capone had a lawyer nicknamed 'Easy Eddie'. He was Capone's lawyer for a good reason. Eddie was very good! In fact, Eddie's skills at legal manoeuvering kept Big Al out of jail for a long time.

To show his appreciation, Capone paid him very well. Not only was the money big, but Eddie got special perks as well. For instance, he and his family occupied a fenced-in mansion with all the conveniences of the day. The estate was so large that it filled an entire Chicago City block.

Eddie lived the high life of Chicago mob and gave little consideration to the atrocities that went on around him. Eddie did have one soft spot, however. He had a son that he loved dearly. Eddie saw to it that his son got best of education and everything he desired. Nothing was withheld.

And, despite his involvement with organised crime, Eddie even tried to teach him right from wrong. Eddie wanted his son to be a better man than he was. Yet, with all his wealth and influence, there were two things he couldn't give his son; he couldn't pass on a good name or a good example.

One day, Easy Eddie reached a difficult decision. He wanted to rectify wrongs he had done. He decided he would go to the authorities and tell the truth about Al 'Scarface' Capone, clean up his tarnished name, and offer his son some semblance of integrity. To do this, he would have to testify against the mob, and he knew that the cost would be great. But he testified.

Within a year, Easy Eddie's life ended in a blaze of gunfire on a lonely Chicago street. But in his eyes, he had given his son the greatest gift he had to offer, at the greatest price he would ever pay.

Story Number Two

World War II produced many heroes. One such man was Lieutenant Commander Butch O'Hare. He was a fighter pilot assigned to the aircraft carrier Lexington in the South Pacific. One day his entire squadron was sent on a mission. After he was airborne, he looked at his fuel gauge and realized that someone had forgotten to top off his fuel tank. He would not have enough fuel to complete his mission and get back to his ship.

His flight leader told him to return to the carrier. Reluctantly, he dropped out of the formation and headed back to the fleet. As he was returning to the mother ship, he saw something that turned his blood cold; a squadron of Japanese Aircraft was speeding its way towards the American Fleet.

The American fighters were gone on a sortie, and the fleet was all but defenseless. He couldn't reach his squadron and bring them back in time to save the fleet. Nor could he warn the fleet of the approaching danger. There was only one thing to do. He must somehow divert the Japenese from the fleet.

Laying aside all thoughts of personal safety, he dove into the formation of Japanese planes. Wing-mounted 50 caliber's blazed as he charged in, attacking one surprised enemy plane and then another. Butch wove in and out of the now broken formation and fired at as many planes as possible until all his ammunition was finally spent.

Undaunted, he continued the assault. He dove at the planes, trying to clip a wing or tail in hope of damaging as many enemy planes as possible, rendering them unfit to fly. Finally, the exasperated Japanese squadron took off in another direction.

Deeply relieved, Butch O'Hare and his tattered fighter limped back to the carrier. Upon arrival, he reported the event. The film from the gun-camera mounted on his plane told the tale. It showed the extent of Butch's daring attempt to protect his fleet. He had, in fact, destroyed five enemy aircraft.

This took place on February 20, 1942, and for that action Butch became the Navy's first Ace of World War II, and the first Naval Aviator to win the Medal of Honor.

A year later Butch was killed in an aerial combat at the age of 29. His home town would not allow the memory of this WW II hero to fade, and today, O'Hare Airport in Chicago is named in tribute to the courage of this great man.

The next time you find yourself at O'Hare International, visit Butch's memorial displaying his statue and his Medal of Honor. It's located between Terminals 1 and 2.

So, what do these two stories have to do with each other?

Butch O'Hare was Easy Eddie's son!

Power of Words

Words have special powers...

The power to create smiles or frowns.

The power to generate laughs or tears.

The power to lift up or put down.

The power to motivate or de-motivate.

The power to teach good or evil.

The power to express love or hate.

The power to give or take.

The power to heal or harm.

Choose your words carefully!

Seasons

There was a man who had four sons. He wanted his sons to learn not to judge things too quickly. So he sent them each on a quest, in turns, to go and look at a pear tree that was a great distance away.

The first son went in winter, the second in spring, the third in summer, and the youngest son in autumn. When they had all gone and come back, he called them together to describe what they had seen.

The first son said that the tree was ugly, bent and twisted. The second son said, no, it was covered with green buds and full of promise. The third son differed; he said it was laden with blossoms that smelled so sweet and looked so beautiful, it was the most graceful thing he had ever seen. The last son disagreed with all of them; he said it was ripe and drooping with fruits, full of life and fulfillment.

The man then explained to his sons that they were all correct, because they had each seen but only one season in the tree's life. He told them that one cannot judge a tree, or a person, by only one season. The essence of who they are and the pleasure, joy and love that comes can only be measured at the end, when all the seasons are up.

If you give up when it's winter, you will miss the promise of your spring, the beauty of your summer, fulfillment of your autumn. Don't let the pain of one season destroy the joy of all the rest. Don't judge life by one difficult season. Persevere through the difficult patches and better times are sure to come some time.

> *Don't hurry, don't worry. You're here only for a short while. So be sure to stop and smell the flowers.*

Limitations

Here's a story about George Dantzig, the famous mathematician, whose contributions to Operations Research and Systems Engineering have made him immortal. As a college student, George studied very hard, often late into the night, so late, that he overslept one morning, arriving twenty minutes late for Professor Neyman's class.

He quickly copied the two math's problems on the board, assuming they were homework assignment. It took him several hours to work through the two problems, but finally he had a breakthrough and dropped the homework on Professor's desk the next day. Six weeks later, on a Sunday morning, his excited professor awakened George at 6 a.m.

Since George was late for class, he hadn't heard the professor announce that the two unsolvable equations on the board were mathematical mind-teasers that even Einstein hadn't been able to solve!

But George Dantzig, working without any thoughts of limitation, had solved not one, but two problems that had stumped mathematicians for thousands of years.

He simply said, "George solved the problems because he didn't know he couldn't."

The fool didn't know it was impossible.

So he did it!

* * *

As per the rules of aerodynamics, the bumblebee can not fly. But it flies, because it does not know the rules of aerodynamics.

Sharpen Your Skills

Once two woodcutters argued, who of them can cut more wood in eight hours.

In the morning both of them took up their positions. First they worked at the same speed. But after an hour, one of them found that the other one had stopped cutting. Realising that this was his chance, the first woodcutter started to cut trees with double vigour.

Ten minutes passed, and he heard that the second woodcutter started to work again. They were working almost synchronously, when the first woodcutter heard that his opponent had stopped again. The first woodcutter continued to work, feeling the smell of victory.

This lasted all day long. Each hour the second woodcutter stopped for ten minutes and the other one continued to work. When time finished, the first woodcutter who had worked without stopping was absolutely sure that he had won the challenge.

He was extremely surprised to know that the other woodcutter had cut more trees.

"How did that happen?" He asked his opponent, "After each hour I heard that you had stopped work for ten minutes. How could you cut more trees than me? It's impossible!"

"It was very simple", replied the second woodcutter, "After every hour I stopped work for ten minutes. And when you were cutting the trees, in those 10 minutes I sharpened my axe."

Every skill you sharpen doubles your odds of success.

What Goes Around Comes Around

In 1892 at Stanford University, an 18-year-old student was struggling to pay his fees. He was an orphan, and not knowing where to turn for money, he came up with a bright idea. He and a friend decided to host a musical concert on campus to raise money for their education.

They reached out to the great pianist Ignacy J. Paderewski. His manager demanded a guarantee fee of $ 2000 for the piano recital. A deal was struck and the boys began to work to make the concert a success.

The big day arrived. But unfortunately, they could not manage to sell enough tickets. The total collection was only $ 1600. Disappointed, they went to Paderewski and explained their plight. They gave him the entire $ 1600, plus a cheque for the balance $ 400. They promised to honour the cheque at the earliest possible.

"No," said Paderewski. "This is not acceptable." He tore up the cheque, returned $ 1600 and told the two boys, "Deduct whatever expenses you have incurred. Keep the money you need for your fees and just give me whatever is left." The boys were overawed, and thanked him profusely.

It was a small act of kindness. But it clearly marked out Paderewski as a great human being. Why should he help two people he did not even know!

We all come across situations like these in our lives. And most of us only think "If I help them, what would happen to me?" The truly great people think, "If I don't help them, what will happen to them?" They don't do it expecting anything in return. They do it because they feel it's the right thing to do.

Paderewski later went on to become the Prime Minister of Poland. He was a great leader, but unfortunately when the

World War began, Poland was ravaged. There were more than 1.5 million people starving in his country, and no money to feed them.

Paderewski did not know where to turn for help. He reached out to the US Food and Relief Administration for help. It was at that time headed by Herbert Hoover, who later went on to become the US President. Hoover agreed to help and quickly shipped tons of food grains to feed the starving Polish people.

A calamity was averted. Paderewski was relieved. He decided to go across to meet Hoover and personally thank him. When Paderewski began to thank Hoover for his noble gesture, Hoover quickly interjected and said, "You shouldn't be thanking me Mr. Prime Minister. You may not remember this, but several years ago, you helped two young students go through college. I was one of them."

The world is a wonderful place. What goes around comes around.

Do you know, why gaps have been created between fingers?

So that someone who is special to you, comes and fills those gaps by holding your hands.

* * *

Smile when picking up the phone. The caller will hear it in your voice.

* * *

Happy the man, and happy he alone

He who can call today his own

He who, secure within, can say

Tomorrow do thy worst, for I have lived today.

Judging a Person

Can you judge who is the best person amongst these three?

Mr A: He had friendship with bad politicians, had two wives, was a chain smoker, and drank throughout the day.

Mr B: He was kicked out of office twice, used to sleep till noon, was a chain smoker, tried opium in college and drank whiskey every evening.

Mr C: He was a decorated war hero, a vegetarian, didn't smoke, didn't drink and never cheated his wife.

You would say ofcourse Mr. C is the best.

But...

Mr A was Franklin Roosevelt, 32nd President of the USA.

Mr B was Winston Churchill, former British Prime Minister.

Mr C was Adolf Hitler!

Strange but true.

It's risky to judge anyone by one's habits. Character is a complex phenomenon. Enjoy the journey called Life.

> *Judging a person does not define who they are. It defines who you are.*
>
> * * *
>
> *While you're hating your life just because you can't get what you want,*
>
> *Remember that someone is praying to have a life like yours.*

Crowd Funding

In 1975, half a million dairy farmers in Gujarat donated two rupees each to help make a movie on their lives. The film was called *Manthan* and it was directed by Shyam Benegal.

When a young Benegal went to Verghese Kurien with the idea of *Manthan*, he flatly refused, stating that his co-operative organisation is not in the business of funding Hindi movies. But Benegal convinced him that this Hindi film would convert more farmers outside of Gujarat to join the milk cooperative movement and make it far bigger than what it currently was.

So Benegal and Kurien came up with the idea of crowdfunding *Manthan* by requesting Rs. 2 donation from each of the 500,000 milk farmers. The farmers were excited that a Hindi film was being made on their lives and readily agreed. *Manthan* raised Rs. 10 lacs in less than a week and Benegal shot the movie in 45 days with actors like Naseer, Smita Patil, Girish Karnad and Amrish Puri. During shooting, all the actors lived in villages of Gujarat like commoners.

When *Manthan* was released, the same 500,000 farmers and their families paid for the tickets and watched the movie in makeshift tents and single screen theatres across Gujarat making it a huge hit. Not just this, Kurien distributed the film for free to teach more farmers about starting cooperatives, sending teams with the movie reels and projectors to 1000s of villages. Millions of farmers watched *Manthan* and the idea of milk cooperatives spread like wildfire across India.

What is special about *Manthan*? *Manthan* is the first-ever crowd-funded movie in the world. From 500,000 farmers, India today has 18 million farmers associated with milk cooperatives, supporting over 80 million rural households with jobs and income. *Manthan* was not just a film, it was a movement that led to transforming India into the largest milk producer in the world.

Indian *Jugaad*

In Japan, in a Soap Manufacturing Company the soap blocks were made, then wrapped in a wrapping paper automatically on an assembly conveyer belt and finally packed in cartons.

Sometimes it happened that the wrapping machine wrapped the paper without soap, i.e., they had an empty packet without soap.

To rectify this problem the Japanese company bought a costly X-ray scanner from US to check on the assembly line whether the packet contained soap and wasn't empty.

A similar problem happened at a big soap manufacturer in India. Guess what they did?

They bought a fan costing around Rs. 1500/- and placed it on the edge of the assembly line.

The empty wrappers without soap just blew away.

In a small Indian village, a farmer's cow was struggling to produce milk. The farmer, being a master of jugaad, came up with a creative solution. He put a pair of headphones on the cow and started playing Bollywood music!

The cow, seemingly enjoying the tunes, began to produce more milk than ever before! The farmer proudly declared, "Music to my cow's ears... and milk to my bucket!"

* * *

If the grass looks greener on the other side...

Stop staring, stop comparing, stop complaining

Start watering the grass you're standing on.

Comparison

Shweta covered a distance of 6 km in one hour.

Akash covered the same distance in one and a half hour.

Which of the two is better and healthier?

Of course our answer will be Shweta.

What if we say that Shweta covered this distance on a prepared track while Akash did it on a sandy path?

Then our answer will be Akash.

But when we come to know that Shweta is 50 years old while Akash is 25 years old?

Then our answer will be Shweta again.

But we also come to know that Akash's weight is 140 kg while Shweta's weight is 65 kg.

Again our answer will be Akash.

As we learn more about Akash and Shweta, our opinions and judgments about who is better will change.

The reality of life is also similar. We form opinions very superficially and hastily, due to which we are not able to do justice to ourselves and others.

Opportunities vary.

Resources differ.

Problems change.

Solutions are different.

Therefore the excellence of life is not in comparing with anyone but in testing oneself.

You are the best. Stay as you are and keep trying your best according to your circumstances.

Healing

John D Rockfeller, born in 1839, was once the richest man in the world, the first billionaire. By age 25, he controlled one of the largest oil refineries in the US. By age 31, he had become the world's largest oil refiner. By age 38, he commanded 90% of the oil refined in US. By 50, he was the richest man in the country. As a young man, every decision was tailored to create his personal power and wealth.

But at the age of 53, he became ill. His entire body became racked with pain and he lost all his hair. In complete agony, the world's only billionaire who could buy anything he wanted, became helpless. He could only digest soup and certain types of biscuits. He could not sleep, would not smile and nothing in life meant anything to him. His personal, highly skilled physicians predicted he would die within a year. That year passed agonisingly slow.

As he approached death, he woke one morning with the vague realisation of not being able to take any of his wealth with him into the next world. The man who could control the business world suddenly realised he was not in control of his own life. He called his attorneys, accountants, and managers and announced that he wanted to channel his assets to hospitals, research, and charity work. He established his Foundation. This new Enterprise eventually led to the discovery of penicillin, cure for malaria, tuberculosis and diphtheria, among many others.

But perhaps the most amazing part of Rockefeller's story is that the moment he began to give back a portion of all that he had earned, his body's chemistry altered so significantly that he got better. It looked as if he would die at 53 but he lived to be 98. Rockefeller learned gratitude and gave back the vast majority of his wealth. Doing so made him whole. It is one thing to be healed. It is another to be made whole.

The Obedient Wife

There was a man, who had worked all his life and saved all his money. He was a real miser when it came to money. Just before he was about to die, he said to his wife, "When I die, I want you to take all my money and put it in the casket with me. I want to take my money to the after-life with me."

And so he got his wife to promise him, with all of her heart. He soon died. He was stretched out in the casket. His wife was sitting there, dressed in black, and her friend was sitting next to her. When they finished the ceremony, and just before the undertaker got ready to close the casket, the obedient wife said, "Wait for just a moment!"

She had a metal box with her, which she put in the casket. Then the undertaker locked the casket down and they rolled it away.

Then her friend said, "Girl, I know you are not foolish enough to put all that money in there with your husband."

The loyal wife replied, "Listen, I'm a wife; I cannot go back on my word I promised him."

"You mean to tell me you put that money in the casket with him?"

"I sure did," said the loyal wife. "I got all the money together, put it into my account, and wrote him a cheque. I put the cheque in the casket. Now it is up to him to encash the cheque. If he can encash it, then he can spend it."

Happiness is not an absence of problems, but an opportunity to deal with them.

* * *

Nothing is permanent in this world, not even our troubles.

The Story of Watermelons

My village is famous for its watermelons. When I was a child, a farmer would organise a watermelon eating contest at the end of the harvest season. All the kids would be invited to eat as many watermelons as they wanted. Years later, I went to study engineering. I went back to my village after several years. I went to the market looking for watermelons. They were all gone. The ones that were there were so small.

I went to see the farmer who hosted the watermelon eating contest. His son had taken over. He would host the contest but there was a difference.

When the older farmer gave us watermelons to eat he would ask us to spit out the seeds into a bowl. We were told not to bite into the seeds. He was collecting the seeds for his next crop. We were unpaid child labourers, actually. He kept his best watermelons for the contest and he got the best seeds which would yield even bigger watermelons the next year.

His son, when he took over, realised that the larger watermelons would fetch more money in the market so he sold the larger ones and kept the smaller ones for the contest.

The next year, the watermelons were smaller, the year later even more small. In watermelons the generation is one year. In seven years, village's best watermelons were finished.

In humans, generations change after 25 years. It will take us more than 100 years to figure what we were doing wrong while educating our children. Unless we employ our best to train the next generation, this is what can happen to us. Each one of us is responsible to offer our best to the next generation!

We do not suffer because we fail to fulfill a false desire. We suffer because we possess the false desire.

The Veblen Effect

At 23, Julius Caesar was a junior politician on the way up. But he had an advantage—confidence and brains. Sailing across the Aegean Sea, he was captured by Sicilian pirates. They demanded a ransom of 500 kg of silver. Caesar told them they were being ridiculous. He couldn't possibly allow himself to be ransomed so cheaply. The pirates hesitated. They were really confused at this suggestion. Caesar insisted the ransom must be raised to 1500 kg of silver. Now the pirates didn't know what to make of this. Normally, their captives tried to escape as cheaply as possible. They didn't understand what was going on. But if he said he would triple the ransom, why argue? They let Caesar's men go back to Rome to raise the money. And in Rome, Caesar suddenly became very famous. No one had ever been ransomed for such a vast sum before. Everybody thought, "He must be very special, he must be incredibly important." That ransom demand put Caesar on the political map. He had just invented the Veblen effect.

The Veblen effect is when consumers perceive higher priced goods to be worth more, simply because they cost more, like Rolex, Louis Vuitton, Christian Dior, Harrods. None of them are actually any better than the cheaper alternatives, but the price alone makes them seem more desirable. Caesar had effectively made himself a Veblen brand. He'd placed a value on himself greater than anyone in Rome. But, as far as anyone knew, it wasn't him who had done it. It was an independent valuation. So it must be true. And because Caesar was now so highly valued, his men had little trouble raising the ransom money. They returned to the island and freed him. So Caesar was now both very rich and very famous. With that same combination of confidence and brain, he became ruler of Rome. And he presided over the golden age of the Roman Empire. Caesar knew that reality begins in the mind. So the most important piece of real estate in which to stake a claim is the human mind.

Leader

In 1947, a powerful nuclear reactor was built in Canada in Ontario at a place called Chalk River Laboratories. It was used mainly for research purposes. One day, about five years into the life of that reactor in December 1952, the reactor exploded because of a combination of human error and mechanical failure, causing the reactor to melt down, which then set off a series of explosions. It is a miracle that no one was hurt, but in 1952 this was still uncharted territory. This meltdown at Chalk River was the world's first nuclear reactor disaster ever. So even though the explosions of the meltdown didn't kill anybody, they were very concerned about what they were going to do with all the radiation and the ongoing threat of the still decomposing reactor. There was no model, no instruction manual for how to clean this thing up. The plant was flooded with radioactive water. The reactor itself was highly radioactive but the whole thing needed to be addressed. It wasn't going to take care by itself, one couldn't just leave it. It needed to be shut down and taken apart and then removed from the site so it wouldn't cause any more destruction.

How do you do this without subjecting the people working on shutdown to a deadly amount of radiation? To figure it out the Canadian government sought help from the US government and specifically from the US Navy. The US Navy by that time had an elite nuclear submarine program, therefore they had a lot of trained engineers who were experienced in nuclear technology.

They knew that anybody working on this shutdown effort could only spend about 90 seconds inside the reactor before they would hit what was considered to be the limit for radiation exposure. They were the best people on Earth to handle this kind of crisis but then they had to make a very specific plan that would split the whole task of taking apart the nuclear reactor. They decided to split the whole thing, everything they needed to do into individual 90-second steps so as to limit radiation exposure. So the way it worked was, one man would run in and like unscrew a bolt if that would take 90 seconds. Then he would run out and the next man would run in for 90 seconds. The next guy would do whatever the next step was, and so on.

In order to plan this to these tiny little increments of time they actually built a full-size replica of the reactor at a nearby playground. Then they practised every single step of shutdown, breakdown and disassembly of the reactor. They practised it all on the replica, that is how they took this thing apart one bolt at a time in 90 second work shift at a time. It sounds insane but it actually worked. The melted down reactor was safely disassembled and removed from the site. The entire thing was actually reassembled and running safely in just a few years.

It was of course a success that came at great risk to the men who had to run into that radioactive reactor to take it apart bit by bit. The man who was in charge of this incredibly risky innovative operation was just 28 years old. He was a Lieutenant in the Navy with nuclear submarine experience. He was one of the only men in the entire world at that time who had the skill-set to develop and execute this kind of plan. He just did not plan it, but himself went down inside the melted down nuclear reactor.

Name of this valiant person was James Earl Carter, or Jimmy in short. While in Navy, he got chosen for the prestigious nuclear submarine program. He commanded the elite team that saved Canada from world's first full-scale nuclear reactor disaster. He himself spent 89 seconds inside the Chalk Point reactor doing his piece of task. He confided later that after the incident his urine tested positive for radioactivity.

The world knows him as Jimmy Carter, 39th President of the USA. He breathed his last on 29th December, 2024 at the ripe age of 100.

Innocence

Every day early morning a little girl would come to the temple and stand before the idol, close her eyes and with folded hands, murmur something for a couple of minutes. Then open her eyes, bow down, smile and go out running. This was a daily routine.

The temple *poojari* used to observe her and was curious about what she was doing. He thought, she is too small to know the deeper meaning of religion, she would hardly know any prayers. But then what was she doing every morning in the temple?

Many days passed and *poojari* now couldn't resist but to find out more about her behaviour. One morning, *poojari* reached there before the girl and waited for her to complete her ritual. He placed his hand on her head and said, "My child, I have seen that you come here regularly. What do you do?"

"I pray," She said spontaneously.

"Do you know any prayers?" asked the *poojari* with some suspicion in his voice.

"... No", replied the girl.

"Then what are you doing closing your eyes, every day?" he smiled.

Very innocently the girl said: "I do not know any prayer, but I know 'a, b, c, d....up to z.' I recite it five times and tell God that I don't know your prayer, but it cannot be outside of these alphabets. Please arrange the alphabets as you wish and that is my prayer." And she ran, jumping on her way out.

The *poojari* stood there dumbstruck, staring at her for a long time as she slowly disappeared running away.

> *A child's heart is God's best abode.*

Take Off Your Blindfold

His dad takes him into the forest, blindfolded, and leaves him. He is required to sit on a stump the whole night and not to take off the blindfold until the rays of sun shine through it. He cannot cry out for help to anyone. Once he survives the night he is a man. He cannot tell the other boys of this experience. Each lad must come into his own manhood.

The boy was terrified and could hear all kinds of noises. Beasts were all around him; maybe even some human would hurt him. The wind blew the grass, and it shook his stump, but he sat stoically, never removing the blindfold. It was the only way he could become a man.

Finally, after a horrific night, the sound of the night disappeared; he could feel the warmth of the sun. He removed his blindfold. It was then that he saw his father sitting on the stump next to him, keeping watch the entire night.

We are never alone. Even when we do not know it, the entire universe is beside us to watch and protect us; all we have to do is to take off our blindfolds.

Mind is nothing but traffic of thoughts. Select your route carefully.

* * *

Life is not measured by the breaths we take, but by the moments that take our breath away.

* * *

When problems seem to be chasing you, don't try to run away. Turn around and face them calmly and confidently, knowing that your inner strength is greater than any outer circumstances.

Solution to a Problem

Many years ago, in a small village, a farmer had the misfortune of owing a large sum of money from a village moneylender. The moneylender, who was old and ugly, fancied the farmer's beautiful daughter. So he proposed a bargain. He said he would forego the farmer's debt if he could marry his daughter. Both the farmer and his daughter were horrified by the proposal.

So the cunning moneylender suggested that they let luck decide the matter. He told them that he would put a black pebble and a white pebble into an empty money bag. Then the girl would have to pick one pebble from the bag.

1. If she picked the black pebble, she would become his wife and her father's debt would be forgiven.
2. If she picked the white pebble she need not marry him and her father's debt would still be forgiven.
3. But if she refused to pick a pebble, her father would be thrown into jail.

They were standing on a pebble strewn path in the farmer's field. As they talked, the moneylender bent over to pick up two pebbles. As he picked them up, the sharp-eyed girl noticed that he had picked up two black pebbles and put them into the bag. He then asked the girl to pick a pebble from the bag.

Now, imagine that you were that girl. What would you have done? If you had to advice her, what would you have told her?

Careful analysis would produce three possibilities:

1. The girl should refuse to take a pebble.
2. The girl should show that there were two black pebbles in the bag and expose the moneylender as a cheat.
3. The girl should pick a black pebble and sacrifice herself in order to save her father from his debt and imprisonment.

Take a moment to ponder over the story. The above story is used with the hope that it will make us appreciate the difference between lateral and logical thinking. The girl's dilemma cannot be solved with traditional logical thinking. Think of the consequences if she chooses the above logical answers.

What would you recommend the girl to do?

Well, here is what she did...

The girl put her hand into the moneybag and drew out a pebble. Without Looking at it, she fumbled and let it fall onto the pebble-strewn path where it immediately became lost among all the other pebbles.

"Oh, how clumsy of me," she said. "But never mind, if you look into the bag for the one that is left, you will be able to tell which pebble I picked."

Since the remaining pebble is black, it must be assumed that she had picked the white one. And since the moneylender dare not admit his dishonesty, the girl changed what seemed an impossible situation into an extremely advantageous one.

Moral: Most complex problems do have a solution. What is needed is to rise one step higher to solve them.

> *The size of your problems is nothing compared with your ability to solve them. Don't overestimate your problems and underestimate yourself.*
>
> * * *
>
> *The mind is a superb instrument if used rightly. Used wrongly, it becomes very destructive. To put it more accurately, it is not so much that we use our mind wrongly—we usually don't use it at all.* ***It uses us!***

Your Lucky Charm

A bus full of passengers was going to its destination. Suddenly the weather changed and there was a huge downpour and lightening all around. They could see that the lightening would appear to come towards the bus and then go elsewhere. After two or three horrible instances of being saved from lightening, the driver stopped the bus about fifty feet away from a pole and said, "We have somebody in the bus whose death is a certainty today. Because of that person everybody else will also get killed. Now listen carefully what I am saying. I want each person to come out of the bus one by one and touch the pole and come back. Whom so ever death is certain will get caught up by the lightening and will die and everybody else will be saved."

They had to force the first person to go and touch the pole and come back. He reluctantly got down from the bus and went and touched the pole. His heart leaped with joy when nothing happened and he was still alive. This continued for rest of the passengers who were all relieved when they touched the pole and nothing happened.

When the last passenger's turn came, everybody looked at him with accusing eyes. That passenger was extremely fearful and reluctant since he was the only one left. Everybody forced him to get down and go and touch the pole. With a 100% fear of death in mind, the last passenger walked to the pole and touched it.

There was a huge sound of thunder and the lightening came down and hit the bus, yes the lightening hit the bus, and killed each and every passenger inside the bus. It was because of the presence of this last passenger, that earlier the entire bus was safe and the lightening could not strike the bus.

Think about it... Look around you. Probably someone is there around you, in the form of your parents, your spouse, your children, your siblings, your friends, etc., who are saving you from harm. You will surely find that person!

Perceptions

It was a beautiful night. Poets lay awake, drawing inspiration from the star spangled sky. Lovers drew closer, gazing at the moon. Children were playing in the moonlight. One man watched all this with increasing despair. He was a thief. If nobody slept, how was he to do what he wanted to do. The entire community was awake. He waited endlessly. Somehow the people of this town were just not sleepy that night. Hours of waiting and strolling around in search of a dark sleeping household made the thief very tired. He lay down under a tree and within seconds, he was fast asleep.

Even the sun's sharp rays failed to rouse the thief from his deep sleep. A drunkard tottered along and seeing the man lying curled up beneath the tree, he muttered: "This guy must be my master. He must have drunk so much that he is still not able to get up. Stupid fellow doesn't know his limit." Another passerby, a gambler, stopped and bent down to check the sleeping man's pockets. "Poor guy!" He thought to himself, "He must have gambled all night to his last paisa. Too bad he didn't know when to stop. His wife wouldn't have let him in the house and so the unfortunate fellow must have fallen asleep here."

The day was gathering momentum. The sun was really sharp and yet the thief was asleep. A few schoolchildren were playing football. A passerby cautioned them, "Look children, there is a man sleeping nearby. Be careful not to disturb him." Having advised the children, the man who was also a thief, went closer to the sleeping man. "He must be a thief like me, who having found nothing all night, is trying to sleep off his frustration."

We saw how one sleeping man evoked so many different reactions. But when we walk into a room full of people, each holding a view different from ours, we find it difficult to accept. Don't you feel that if we consider perspectives of others before coming to a rational decision, life will be so much better.

Another Way to Solve a Problem

Ever since Aarav was a child, he had a fear of someone under his bed at night. So he went to a psychiatrist and told him, "I've a problem. Every time I go to bed I think there's somebody under it. I'm scared. I think I'm going crazy."

"Just put yourself in my hands for a few weeks", said the psychiatrist. "Come talk to me three times a week and we should be able to get rid of these fears."

"How much do you charge?"

"Two thousand rupees per session", replied the doctor.

"I'll sleep on it and if needed I will come back to you", Aarav replied.

Six months later he met the psychiatrist on the road. "Why didn't you come to see me about those fears you were having?" he asked.

"Well, two thousand rupees a visit, three times a week, for a few weeks is an awful lot of money. A carpenter cured me for 500 rupees."

"Is that so!" With a bit of an attitude he said, "And how, may I ask, did the carpenter cure you?"

"He cut the legs of the bed. There is nobody under the bed now!"

Mind is a superb instrument if used rightly. It is not so much that we use our mind wrongly—we usually don't use it at all. It uses us!

* * *

The happiness of your life depends on the quality of your thoughts.

Whom will You Salute

When Dr. Abdul Kalam was President, he visited Coonoor. On reaching, he came to know that Field Marshall Sam Manekshaw was in Military Hospital there. Dr. Kalam went to meet him, enquired about his health and asked Sam, "Are you comfortable? Is there anything I can do? Do you have any grievance or any requirement that would make you more comfortable?" Sam said, "Yes Your Excellency, I have one grievance." With concern and anguish, Kalam asked him what it was. Sam replied, "Sir, my grievance is that I am not able to get up and salute the most respected President of my beloved country." Kalam held Sam's hand as both were in tears. But Sam did tell APJ that he was not paid the pension of the Field Marshall's rank till then, for nearly twenty years. An aghast President went to Delhi and passed the pension with arrears within a week and sent the cheque of nearly Rs. 1.3 crores to Sam. That was the greatness of APJ. But then Sam received the cheque and promptly donated it to the Army Relief fund. Whom will you salute now?

A young officer was on his round when one of the riflemen did not notice him and missed saluting him. The youngster got cheesed off and summoned the Gorkha and asked him the reason for not saluting him. The Gorkha innocently replied that he did not see 'Lieutenant Huzoor'. The youngster, not convinced, punished the Gorkha to a thousand salutes. The soldier immediately started saluting. A senior officer was passing by and asked the youngster as to what was happening. The youngster said, "Sir, this soldier had the audacity of not saluting me. So I have punished him with 1000 salutes." The officer replied, "Bloody good punishment young man, but ensure that you return each of his salutes." For the next two hours the unit was treated to a scene of a Gorkha saluting and the young officer returning each of his salutes.

Cracked Pot

A water bearer had two large pots, each hung on the ends of a pole which he carried across his neck. One of the pots had a crack in it, while the other pot was perfect and always delivered full portion of water. At the end of the long walk from the stream to the house, the cracked pot arrived only half full.

For a full two years this went on daily, with the bearer bringing only one and a half pots full of water to his house. Of course, the perfect pot was proud of its accomplishment. The poor cracked pot was ashamed of its own imperfection, and miserable that it was able to accomplish only half of what it had been made to do. After two years of what it perceived to be a bitter failure, it spoke to the water bearer one day by the stream, "I am ashamed of myself, because this crack in my side causes water to leak out all the way back to your house."

The bearer said to the pot, "Did you notice that there were flowers only on your side of the path, but not on the other pot's side? That's because I have always known about your flaw, and I planted flower seeds on your side of the path. Every day while we walk back, you've watered them. I have been able to pick these beautiful flowers to decorate the table. Without you being just the way you are, there would not be this beauty to grace the house."

Moral: Each of us has our own unique flaws. We're all cracked pots. But it's the cracks and flaws we each have that make our lives together so very interesting and rewarding.

> *You are not fully dressed ...*
>
> *If you do not smile.*

The Red Bike Moment

When a 12-year-old boy had his new red bicycle stolen in 1954, he sought out a man that he'd heard could help him fill out a police report. That man, Joe Elsby Martin, was a police officer and an amateur boxing trainer.

It was a rainy October night, and the boy had tears in his eyes when he spoke to Martin. The boy kept on saying he's gonna whup the punk who stole his bike; to which the cop advised, "if you're gonna whup anyone, you'd better learn how to fight first before challenging people." Martin introduced the boy to boxing through that chance encounter.

The young boy took his advise, and as the old saying goes, 'the rest is history!' That conversation launched the boxing career of the boy, then known as Cassius Clay, who would go on to become an Olympic gold medalist, a three-time world heavy-weight boxing champion, and 'The Greatest' to ever 'float like a butterfly and sting like a bee' Muhammad Ali.

Much of Ali's physical toughness came as a result of his mental toughness and a desire to conclusively prove he was indeed 'the Greatest'. It is pure psychology and the stuff that only legends are made of.

For Ali, that was his "Red Bike Moment"—a turning point in his life. The stolen bike introduced him to Martin, who introduced him to boxing. Ali began training at the gym and just six years later, won Olympic gold.

Most of us can reflect on our own personal history and identify a transformational event in our lives that occurred because of a challenge or some type of adversity. Was there a time when challenging circumstances led to a positive change in your life? Do you have a Red Bike Moment?